Platinum Keys

Personal Power Through Imagination

Sonja A. Smith

American Literary Press, Inc.
Five Star Special Edition
Baltimore, Maryland

Platinum Keys

Library of Congress
Cataloging in Publication Data
ISBN 1-56167-571-7

Library of Congress Card Catalog Number:
99-091136

Published by

American Literary Press, Inc.
Five Star Special Edition
8019 Belair Road, Suite 10
Baltimore, Maryland 21236

Manufactured in the United States of America

For Daddy
My bridge over troubled water

Contents

Introduction

Between minimum and maximum there lies a level called mediocrity, which unfortunately seems to be the accepted maximum of most. As a result, too many of us are comfortable with simply existing and going through the motions of life, as dictated to us by circumstances and the influences of the world. Too many of us, beginning from childhood, have learned well to become followers of this world rather than masters of our own minds. For too many of us, fallacious perceptions have become rooted in our thinking and have produced nothing but dysfunctionalism.

It is true that not until Jehovah God fulfills his promise of a restored paradise here on earth, that we can ever hope to attain perfection. However, for as long as we still exist in this victimizing and oppressive world, we must each aim to make the most of our common senses in order to become more advanced and so better able to resist the world's negative influences.

Because the challenges we meet in life are varied and complex, it can never be enough for us to just think linearly or straightforwardly. We must teach ourselves to think in a more advanced way; in length, breadth and depth so to speak. Doing this will help us to have more of a bird's eye-view of life and less of an ant's.

I am sure you agree that life is bad enough as it is for us to add to it more dysfunctionalism. We have more than enough emotionally disoriented, confused, misled and victimized persons all around us. So, as far as our imperfect state will allow us, why not let us see if we can make a difference, if even a small one? Why not let us see if we can become one of the relatively few people who are emotionally regulated, accurately perceptive, happy and positive? This is certainly something worth striving for. So how can we proceed?

Well, trained psychologists and counselors have plenty to say. Yet, it is said that many of them offer more confusion than anything else. Most times, all that are needed for one to advance are fresh perspectives based on elementary insight, supplemented with appropriate adjustments. That, rather than the superfluous intellect and the complex philosophies that are so commonly sought. A certain level of independence is necessary as well since it is important for us to believe that we do not need to depend on the world to decide for us how we should think or live.

As human beings, we should each assume the responsibility of seeing to it that our choices, habits and personalities are ones that have a positive effect on *our* lives and on the people in them. We should all seek to be assets rather than liabilities to ourselves and others, sources of joy rather than sources of burden.

Fortunately, we do not have to be brilliant or be endowed with special enlightenment to be successful at this. All that is needed is the desire to advance, insight on our tendencies and capabilities, along with a healthy passion and respect for life and humanity. And more than likely, these are what *Platinum Keys* will help you to develop.

Throughout *Platinum Keys* I have sought to discuss some very sensitive, challenging and thought provoking issues. As a result, I have found the writing of this book to be deeply stimulating, therapeutic even, as it has gently but profoundly inculcated in me some vital gems of wisdom. It is my sincere hope that you will thus find the reading of *Platinum Keys* to be equally stimulating and beneficial. You will find that some of the ideas expressed in it may not necessarily be new, however, I have endeavored to take unique approaches to matters in a way I think will be appealing to you.

I want you to enjoy this book. I want you to continue learning more. I want you to seriously take to heart the responsibility of personal advancement and to reap the wonderful rewards of doing so. And as for me; I want to waltz endlessly in the well-lit ballroom of life's awareness. I can now hear the music starting -- may I have this dance?

Chapter One

Identifying And Acknowledging Your Needs

Before any of us can begin to try to enhance ourselves we must first determine what of us requires enhancement, right? Logically thinking, if there is something about us that needs to be improved it must be due to something lacking in our lives. Something we need to gain more insight on in order to change. Essentially, it must be due to some unfulfilled need. Determining and understanding our unfulfilled needs are the first steps toward self- improvement. The next step being, of course for us to fulfill them.

In this introductory chapter, we will zero in on some primary needs of us humans. I want you to read about them carefully and see if any of them, if even slightly, applies to you. Doing this will open up your channels of awareness and make you better able to absorb exactly what you need and ignore what you don't from the discussions presented throughout this book.

According to the well-known *Maslow's Hierarchy of Needs* five main human needs are:

» **Self Actualization**

» **Self Esteem**

» **Social Needs**

» **Safety (or security) Needs**

» **Physiological Needs**

Take a look at each of them and see if you can identify any unfulfilled need of yours.

Self-Actualization

Each of us as human beings, possesses different attributes, special qualities. We all have room to grow as individuals and to achieve more as we grow. This is where the need for self-actualization comes in. One may feel the need to strive for self-development, self- identity, stimulation and challenge. He (or she) may feel the need to discover his truest potential and to build on it in order to convert it into personal success. He may want to reach out and experience different facets of life, sometimes even doing risky things; as long as it means moving to higher levels of satisfaction and growth. He wants to move from feeling like he is merely existing or just going through the motions of life to feeling like he is actually living a fulfilling, exciting, satisfying, precious life.

A person with a need for self-actualization may:

» Be in a job that requires no particular skill on his part.

» Be stuck in an inflexible routine that does not allow for personal growth.

» Fantasize constantly about what he thinks his ideal life should be like.

» Feel inferior to those who seem not to suffer from this problem.

» Become either very shy, or very outrageous.

» Harbor anger and resentment for life.

» Suffer from television addiction.

» Tend to identify himself with fictitious characters or superstars and 'live' through them.

» Feel the need to prove himself to others.

» Feel oppressed, stifled and painfully frustrated.

» Have a tendency to envy successful people.

» Develop low self-esteem.

Self-Esteem

Having the need for self-esteem means wanting to feel good about your *true* self. It means that you want to genuinely appreciate at least most aspects of yourself. You want to have confidence in your own ability to enrich your life and the lives of others. You want to be deemed as competent and valuable both by yourself and by others around you.

A person with a need for self-esteem may:

» Not like the way he (or she) appears but may make no effort to change.

» Feel like he is of no consequence to the world.

» Tend to idolize more out-going persons.

» Tend to be possessive of other persons, sometimes even falling into obsession.

» Constantly put down himself and others.

» Be obnoxious, overly critical or may gossip habitually.

» Be overly sensitive or suspicious of others' comments or actions, always thinking they have something to do with him.

» Always be on the defensive.

» Believe that he cannot change and so does not make the effort to. He may say something like: "That's just how I am and I can't help but to be that way."

» Find it hard to say 'no' to others.

» Be fearful of ever being in the spotlight, though he may desire the individual attention of others.

» Develop addictions or compulsions.

» Become obsessed with acquiring expensive material things.

» Have social needs.

Social Needs

As is said, we humans are social beings and as such we all have social needs. We all want to feel loved and as though we belong. We want to feel like an important part of a group, whether it is a family, a team, a club et cetera. We want to feel appreciated, accepted, wanted and respected. We want to socialize by being able to express ourselves freely without being ignored or considered odd. We want to do these things because it is the only way that we ourselves can be inclined to give our love, respect and appreciation to others. A person with social needs may:

» Feel lonely and as though no one understands him (or her).

» Want to be a part of a group; even if it means joining a club or a gang.

» Try to be like others instead of his true self, as long as it means fitting in.

» Try by all means to become popular.

» Become materialistic, since his things might draw some needed attention.

- » Dislike being alone for even short periods of time.
- » Yearn to attend social gatherings but when he does so, becomes shy and socially disoriented.
- » Become painfully anxious when having to deal with groups of people.
- » Feel a deep need to intimately connect with another human being.
- » Fantasize constantly about being popular or being the center of attention.
- » Become depressed if not invited to a social gathering.
- » Have safety or security needs.

Safety (or security) Needs

There is the need in us humans for physical and psychological safety or security. We want to feel protected and not threatened in any way. We want to, as best as we can, know what the future holds for us so that we may be prepared and not unpleasantly surprised. We are suspicious of change or differences and we strive to control anything that may disturb our comfort zone or threaten our well-being. We want to feel sure of ourselves and of our ability to succeed in all aspects of our lives. We want to be convinced that we will *always* be needed. A person with safety or security needs may:

» Easily become fearful or anxious.

» Feel suspicious of or threatened by change.

» Always feel as though something is missing in his (or her) life.

» Feel inadequate, unprepared or out of control.

» Constantly seek reassurance from those around him that he is valued and that his life has meaning.

» Have difficulty with trusting others.

» Develop a dependency on more secure persons.

» Work laboriously to acquire wealth, seeking security in material things.

» Carry a weapon and feel as though he is naked without it.

» Manipulate others in attempts to control them so that they will conform to the way *he* wants things to be.

- Constantly seek to be in a romantic relationship or in the company of others, dreading the idea of being alone.
- Have spiritual needs.

Physiological Needs

The physical aspect of the human being of course has very important needs. Physiological needs, such as the need for food, water, shelter and air are life sustaining and the degree of the satisfaction of these needs, since they determine our state of health, can determine greatly our ability to function effectively in all the other aspects of our life. Our bodies are naturally programmed by our Creator to respond urgently to these needs in order to maintain our physical health and so preserve our lives.

Spiritual Needs

This need is a vital one to all humans, which unfortunately Mr. Maslow failed to mention.

The continued proliferation of thousands of different religious organizations is proof alone that man has an innate desire to worship and connect with a higher being. Fortunately, if this need is truly met, that is, if a person comes to serve our Creator in the way that *He* requires, then all the needs mentioned by Maslow can be met to a degree higher than any we can ever attain on our own.

In Conclusion

If you could identify at least *one* need that you desire to be met, then you are, as of right now, on your way to personal advancement. Nothing is wrong with having needs. We all do. What is wrong is when we have a need, have access to the tools needed to meet it and then fail to make the effort to utilize those tools.

Even though I will not be discussing *direct* aids to meeting these specific needs, you will find that as you read on to the following discussions, you will be able to identify for yourself specific tools that you may need in order to meet one or more of your unfulfilled needs.

You are now 'on your mark' in the marathon to personal advancement. Now I want you to get set. Are you ready? Go!

Chapter Two

Platinum Keys To Emotional Orientation

Picture in your mind's eye a crowded street or a busy shopping mall; noisy vendors on a sidewalk; wealthy persons dining and socializing in a quiet fancy restaurant. Picture construction workers on a building site; doctors in offices; a group of morticians; clowns in a circus. Picture the people you work or go to school with; persons in your own family; men, women and children. Can you do that? Great. Now picture some of those same persons from the crowded street angrily honking their car horns at other motorists and pedestrians who in turn hurl cutting remarks in their defense. Picture some of those same wealthy persons from the restaurant, at their homes being victims of physical or emotional abuse from their spouses, being deeply depressed, worried, anxious and constantly visiting their mental health therapists. Picture some of those same doctors, construction workers and even people you think you know well experiencing feelings of fear and sadness even to the point of having suicidal thoughts. Can you picture that? My guess is that you can because these are things that we can all as human beings relate to. In fact, the only reason that we have to picture any of these experiences is because none of us are omnipresent or are the flies on the walls of the homes of other people.

This reality draws our attention to a distinct common thread running through the fabric of human society regardless of race, sex, class, age, wealth, or occupation -- emotional disorientation. This is the apparent inability to instinctively understand and hence bridle our feelings. It is the tendency to unwittingly nurture our negative emotions. It results from the failure to manipulate our reasoning abilities with a view to managing our feelings positively and meaningfully. Instead, an emotionally disoriented person will easily give in to his raw feelings and act on them.

Emotional disorientation may be used to explain the tendency in many of us to be easily saddened, angered, or fearful. It may explain the millions of broken relationships, the endless appointments made to see psychologists and councilors, the high levels of emotional sensitivity and anxiety in many of us. Emotional disorientation may also be used to explain the easy eruption of arguments and fights even between close friends, obsession, so called crimes of passion, sleeping disorders, masturbation and sexual promiscuity, poor eating habits and so poor health maintenance, even substance addictions.

'So' you may ask, 'isn't it only human to feel anger, fear, sadness and so on?' Why yes, but it is self-destructive to easily give in to such emotions or to nurture them in ourselves.

Another question that may be asked is: is it really possible for any human being to most times exercise emotional control? Again the answer is yes. These are emotionally oriented people and they do exist. What are they like? Well first I will tell you what they are *not* like.

They are not like persons who appear to be void of emotion, impassive or constantly in a state of serenity. They are not immune to annoyances, irritations, disappointments or feelings of deep concern. They are not superficial. They are not complainers or worriers. They are not miserable persons always blaming others for their misfortunes nor do they depend on others to make them happy. They are not impatient. Instead, emotionally oriented persons are pleasant, positive, and usually compassionate. They have healthy senses of humor and they always try to make the best of any situation. They are not easily angered or saddened but are happy and self-fulfilled. They are confident, independent and tend to be insightful. They are appreciative of many facets of life and are enthusiastic and creative in their approach to living. They are non-pretenders and most times courageous. They remain calm and reserved even under provocation or strain.

All this sounds like a wonderful description of a person doesn't it? Maybe even like a fictitious character. But for any of us to match such a description is not an impossibility.

Just as how most of us have the capacity for mental and physical prowess, there exists the capacity for emotional prowess as well. Unfortunately though, in many cases, people fail to invest the time and energy needed to develop this kind of wellness, accepting emotional disorientation as being normal; subconsciously dwelling on the erroneous reasoning that it is only human to be easily emotional. But so far we have learned that it is not 'only human.' It is neurotic and self-destructive.

All That Is Needed

The fact that you are continuing to read this chapter may indicate that you already have the first thing needed to achieve emotional orientation. That is, the interest and the desire to enhance yourself emotionally. This desire means that you recognize that you may be in need of adjustments to your emotional system. This is good, because this recognition is what will open your sense of awareness in order for you to make the precise adjustments needed to become more emotionally oriented.

Along with this desire though, there are other qualities that are necessary for one to be successful. Qualities such as patience, reasonableness and humility. Also, diligence, discernment and sufficient levels of self-esteem and maturity. Just in case you are right now thinking "but I don't have many of these qualities," do not let that be your concern now. All this is being said not for you to judge your level of capability but only to bring forth the awareness that acquiring emotional orientation is no quick and easy undertaking. As with everything else, no one can just decide to be emotionally oriented and then overnight become that way. It takes wisdom, insight, consistent effort, a little practice and time.

Now that we've recognized more or less what is needed, let us now explore some simple and creative tactics that may be used to cultivate emotional orientation. Take your time when reading these and think about each of them very carefully.

To Be or Not To Be? That is the Answer

One of the most powerful attributes of a human being is his ability to choose. Choice, when intelligently exercised can be a saving grace in most of life's sticky situations. In almost all aspects of the human experience, choice is what determines the outcome and the emotional aspect is certainly no exception. Consciously and subconsciously, this fact must be believed and accepted in the mind of anyone who wishes to take advantage of this gift of choice. Yes, you can exercise power over your own person -- to be or not to be -- angry, sad, upset, afraid and so on. You must know that *if you want to* the ball can always be in your court, so to speak, and so you and only you are the one who is responsible at all times for the way you feel. Let's look at a simple example that illustrates the power of choice.

> *Imina Hurry woke up late and so is also running late for work, where an important client is waiting for her. As a result, she rushes to get dressed, barely has a bite to eat, grabs her bag and is out the door. When outside she realizes she doesn't have her car keys. She rushes back inside to the usual car key spot but does not find them there. She searches and searches pulling things out of place and tossing things around. Still the keys are nowhere to be found. Her patience wears thin, soon to be no more and so now she starts throwing things, slamming doors and yelling, 'where the heck did those darn keys go?' (as if the keys just got up that morning and decided to play hide and seek). At this point she has almost totally lost it. She is angry. Angry at the alarm clock for not 'remembering' to go off, angry with*

herself for being late, angry at the keys, angry at the car for needing keys, angry at the mess she has made around the house that she will have to clean up later; angry at the dog for being in the calm, unperturbed state that she is not, angry at her job, at life and at just about everything that will come her way that day. She eventually gives up the search and breaks down in tears.

Now just next door lives Joy Calm. On this same morning she is also running late for work, coincidentally for the same reason. She too rushes to get dressed, grabs a quick bite and is out the door when she realizes she doesn't have her keys. She rushes back inside, checks the usual spots but -- no keys. Now what does she *do? Unlike Miss Hurry, Miss Calm decides to slow down. She uses her intelligence to try to figure out where she might have put them. While tracing her steps, she eats that other slice of toast that she left behind, so at the same time finishes her breakfast. Because she is searching intelligently she need not tear the place apart, so everything around her remains relatively in order.*

When she realizes that she still has not found the keys and that time is running out, she

> ***simply calls her workplace. She briefly and respectfully explains her setback and assures her boss that she will be there as soon as is reasonably possible. While she does feel annoyed at the fact that she is late because she misplaced her keys, she remains calm and continues to search meaningfully for them.***

In this illustration, both these women were faced with the same problem. However, one got to work half an hour late, happy, organized, not to mention filled, while the other one got to work one and a half hours late miserable, confused, hungry, worried about explaining her lateness to her waiting client and yes -- still angry.

The differences in the outcomes of these experiences reveal that choice is a major factor when dealing with potentially emotional situations. Imina Hurry *chose* to give in to her initial annoyance by the inconvenience and allowed it to evolve into anger that eventually made her into an emotional wreck. On the other hand, Joy Calm, though equally annoyed by the inconvenience, chose to act logically and intelligently rather than irrationally and emotionally. She was equally aware of the time that was passing and had the same sense of urgency as did Imina, but she did not waste her time by randomly searching for the keys nor did she choose to panic about being late. Instead, she acted sensibly and responsibly with a keen interest in preserving her patience and self-control.

This situation illustrates a typical example of any potentially emotional experience. In all of these, we can choose how best we will deal with the given circumstance while still maintaining our self-control and peace of mind. We should at all times take responsibility for our own feelings and decide whether we will give in to them or not.

What I sometimes do whenever I'm faced with a potentially emotional situation is to imagine myself at an intersection. Leading from the intersection there are different roads called 'Anger,' 'Sadness,' 'Fear,' 'Anxiety' and so on. Whenever I begin feeling say annoyed or irritated, I see myself being prodded down to the starting line of the road of 'Anger.' Then *right away* I imagine myself rejecting that path and making the choice to take a more positive road. So in that case I tell myself: 'To Go or Not to Go? That is the Answer.'

However you decide to train yourself is entirely up to you. Once you recognize that *you do* have the authority to take responsibility for your feelings, you will become more aware of how you choose to feel or choose to respond in any potentially emotional situation. It is entirely up to you. The choice is always yours.

How Do You Think?

Emotions are aroused primarily due to some thought or pattern of thinking. So if you have negative thoughts such as angry, fearful or depressing thoughts then automatically your emotional system will produce the feelings that correspond to those thoughts.

With this understanding, you should be moved to become more aware of your thinking tendencies. You might need to check to see that your pattern of thinking is based on reasoning that is sound and insightful and not fallacious or illogical. (We'll talk more about fallacious thinking later on).

Whenever you find yourself in a situation where an undesired emotion is being aroused in you, it is important for you to immediately arrest your thought process as it relates to the situation. One effective way to do this is to immediately tell yourself in an undertone: "I despise this feeling. It is not for me. I am going to think about something else." This will help you to turn on to a different frequency so to speak and so rearrest your self-control.

Also, avoid what I like to call the Think Too Much Syndrome. This is the tendency to think unnecessarily about something, laboring over it for long periods. It is common especially for intellects to experience this mental insomnia but just about anyone can suffer from it. Similarly, this form of obsessive prolonged thinking must be *immediately arrested* if we are to maintain emotional orientation.

Make Humor Your Sixth Sense

He who tickles himself may laugh when he pleases.

German proverb

Good humor makes all things tolerable
– Henry Ward Beecher

The cultivating and exercising of a healthy sense of humor is an extremely powerful antidote for the sickness of emotional disorientation. In fact, for many cases it may be all that is needed to begin developing a healthy emotional system.

What exactly, though, is a healthy sense of humor? It is the ability to use one's creative imagination to mentally manipulate an idea, whether brought about by a situation, experience, comment, or otherwise, in order to produce an amusing thought. It is the ability to stimulate amusement or to create laughter, to derive pleasure even from the most uncomfortable and difficult situations. It is the ability to shine if even inwardly in the darkest of moments.

This does not mean that a person with a healthy sense of humor practices making jokes even about very serious matters, insensitively disregarding the feelings of others. He does not wear a silly grin all the time nor is he constantly laughing or being amused by everything he sees or hears, in which case his sense of humor could not be regarded as a healthy one.

Persons possessing a healthy sense of humor tend to be more positive, creative, flexible and less sensitive to life's rough spots. These people are better able to absorb shock or to endure trials than people who do not exercise their senses of humor. The reason for this lies in the principle that it is better for one to destroy the body than to destroy the mind and since the sense of humor helps to protect the mind, a person exercising one remains stronger and better able to endure his trials than a person who does not.

It is said that negative emotions manipulate the immune system making it weak and less efficient. It stands to reason then that the converse is true. In fact, researchers have claimed that positive emotions, which usually enable laughter, can empower the immune system making a person healthier and more resistant to illnesses.

So unlock and improve your God-given sense of humor and make it a dominant part of your personality. You can only have fun exercising it and there are only benefits to be derived. Choose to rid yourself of the pains of taking yourself and life too seriously and avoid persons who do so. You can only be a better person for it. As one poet Langston Hughes puts it: "Like a welcome summer rain, humor may suddenly cleanse and cool the earth, the air and you."

When Procrastination Becomes Your Personal Guardian

Pretending to hold off till a future time your reactions to aroused negative emotions is a neat little trick that you can use to control yourself emotionally.

Let's say for instance that someone says something unkind to you. Something that really arouses in you a feeling of irritation or even hurt. To employ this method you can quickly tell yourself: "Okay now, I am feeling upset and also the need to express it, but what I'll do for now is to act normally and as though it did not happen and then *later* I will express myself." Telling yourself this, or something to this effect, might just be enough to give you the sense of control that you will especially need at that time.

Really though, the best part of doing this is that by the time you are given the opportunity to 'safely' express your emotions, you may not at all feel in the mood to do so. You may have already felt a sense of resolve, trivializing your would-be offender's comment by not responding to it at the time it was made. Simply, that 'later' may never come.

Create the Right Environment

Look around your home or your area of personal space. Believe it or not, its state can have a lot to do with your capability for emotional orientation. If it's messy, disorganized, smelly, dark, stuffy, hot or dull, this can subconsciously affect you and make you less able to maintain your joy and self-control.

So as far as it is possible for you, make sure that your surroundings are conducive to emotional calm and stability. Make it clean, fresh, bright, cheery and at a comfortable temperature. Add your personal unique touch to it and surround yourself with things that amuse you or that bring you comfort or pleasure.

A Hungry Man Is an Angry Man

Avoid hunger as much as you can. Maintain a habit of eating regularly and healthily. Prolonged hunger can be a great contributor to emotional disorientation as it makes such a person more prone to irritations and annoyances and so to anger and frustration.

So, even if it means carrying around a light healthy snack on your person, do what you must to avoid remaining hungry for long periods.

Avoid the Highly Strung

Like the lyrics of a popular song or like the common cold, emotions can be very contagious. Even to the most oriented of us. With this in mind, make a conscious effort to avoid spending regular, prolonged periods with anyone who constantly displays negative, self-destructive emotions. These people come in all forms. They are panic peddlers, worriers, guilt trippers, depressants, complainers, and nervous wrecks. Not only will the effect of these people's emotional disorders affect your behavior, but it will drain you emotionally as well. These sorts of people can be like bloodsucking leeches and if you allow them to, they will suck you emotionally dry. So for as long as it is possible for you, try as best to stay out of their way altogether.

Does this guy remind you of anyone you know?

Just suppose though that you live with such a person or are in a position that makes it impossible for you to physically avoid him, there *is* something you can do. Detach yourself *emotionally* from this person. Distance yourself with regards to your feelings toward him. While you will deal with him politely, respectfully even lovingly, whenever he gets into one of his 'fits', always remain ever conscious of the fact that this is a person who needs help. This is a person who is emotionally ill, and you need to protect yourself from his virus by not committing emotionally to him. Do not think that because you might be more emotionally oriented than he is, that it is your duty to tolerate his behavior or to volunteer therapy for him. Forget that. It is only your duty to protect yourself from the disease of emotional disorientation.

The Power of Music

Music has tremendous power. One issue of *Awake!* magazine stated that "indeed it can play on the gamut of human emotions -- from sadness and pathos to love and joy. Music can lull one into calmness and incite one to rage. It can inspire devotion and promote decadence." Yes, music can seriously influence the mind and so the emotions. Knowledge of this fact then, should move you to be very careful in your choices of it.

If you want to develop and maintain emotional orientation and even your general health, it is helpful for you to listen to music that is not only melodious and rhythmic but upbuilding as well. Music that positively stimulates you. Music that excites pleasure but that also creates good thoughts. Music that will leave you with a sense of satisfaction and encouragement. Music that will massage your mind to relaxation and calm. Music that will empower your soul.

Exhale More Than Just CO_2

Whenever you find yourself becoming negatively emotional, as mentioned before, arrest your thought process immediately. Then, stop whatever you are doing and take three very long, slow breaths. As you inhale, imagine that comfort, calm and control are rushing into your system strengthening and encouraging you. As you exhale, imagine the anger, fear, anxiety or whatever negative emotion you are experiencing, steadily leaving your system, while being replaced by the positive qualities you 'inhaled.'

Focus on the Here and Now

Avoid thinking about something that happened in the past that may have made you annoyed, guilty, hurt or disappointed. Dwelling on such memories can only generate in you destructive negative emotions. Also, avoid dwelling on thoughts of future events that you think may make you anxious, angry, or fearful. The bottom line is: Always keep focused on the *here and now,* being constantly aware of what you are *presently* doing and feeling, not on how you felt before or might feel later. Remember, your present moments can either be loved -- or lost -- and the choice is always yours.

Make Yourself Barren to the Breeding of Obsession

Obsession, insanity, 'tomayto', 'tomaato' it's the same thing. If you have ever experienced obsession (particularly with someone of the opposite sex) or know someone who has, you know that it is a very painful and emotionally debilitating illness.

The subject of obsession is very intricate and complex and admittedly, not one I am prepared to discuss in detail. However I will proceed to mention a few things that we can do in order to make ourselves less susceptible to this disorder.

1. If you are one who suffers from low self-esteem, the need for self-fulfillment, loneliness, insecurity, or if you feel like there is an emotional void in your life, you are without a doubt a possible candidate for obsession. It is some deep need in the heart of a person that serves as the soil for the vine of his obsession. So, if you see where you suffer from any of these problems, addressing them now would be a good idea.

2. Even if you are someone with relatively high self-esteem, do your best to avoid anyone you find attractive who puts you down. Why? Well one very common way for someone to control another, even to the point of leading him to obsession, is to insidiously rob him (or her) of his self-esteem and slowly, teasingly give it back to him. I'll explain to you how this method works. Well first, this potential victimizer will appear to mean you well but at the same time he or she will say or do things to put you down. Then you, without realizing it,

begin to feel that you need to always be doing things to meet the approval or keep the attention of this person. Whenever he approves and says something nice, you feel a sense of satisfaction and joy. Whenever he disapproves and says something negative, you immediately feel low, insecure, and anxious. (It is at this point that he starts to take control of you.) You feel you need to regain that joy again so you do whatever you can to regain this person's approval. You hate the pain, you enjoy the satisfaction. And in your mind, that is by now infected, that satisfaction can only possibly come from him. No one else. You 'need' him. You 'love' him. You want only him. You become obsessed with him.

3 Most of us have, somewhere in our minds, a description or profile of what we deem to be the 'perfect' person. Now let us say you meet someone of the opposite sex whom you find very attractive. What you must be careful of, is comparing and associating this person with your mentally custom-made ideal person. Do not use your mind to build on this person, what really might not be there. This way you will prevent yourself from overestimating the attractiveness of this person. You will be more concerned about who he *really* is and not what he simply *represents* in your mind.

4 If you think you have a tendency to be jealous, demanding, or if you just have difficulty letting go of things, give attention to these problems with a conscious view to getting rid of or at the very least controlling them.

5 If you think you may already be obsessed with someone, get help immediately before things get ugly. Talk to someone mature and trustworthy about your thoughts and feelings toward this person. Do not keep him (or her) a secret in your mind, it will only get worse.

Before I close on this subject, here is a word of advice. If *you* ever happen to become the object of someone's obsession, do not take it lightly and do not interpret it as a complement. Let the person know that you are not comfortable with his (or her) excessive attention and despite his reaction, cut off all unnecessary association with him immediately. If he requests that you help him to deal with it, recognize that you are not in a position to do so. If you can, refer him to someone who is and promptly dismiss yourself from his life. Believe me, you'll be glad you did.

Knowing When and How to Yield

On the highway, or should I say low-way of negative emotions, there are times when the needed **STOP** sign just won't remain standing. This can happen after a long, difficult and demanding day. It can happen after a grave disappointment or a shocking experience. Or, it can happen simply when you are overwhelmed by life, by a bad memory or by an ongoing frustration. At times like those you may feel helpless, angry or just emotionally exhausted and there becomes an instant need for relief.

So then, since the **STOP** sign refuses to stand up, what might a person do? Well, simply put, he may just have to yield to them, yes, give those feelings the right of way. I know some experts may say that at those times you should just grab hold of yourself and control your feelings but unfortunately for us imperfect human beings it doesn't always work that way. There will be times when we will need to have our feelings expressed or at least to have the negative energy channeled somewhere.

I am not here saying that there are times when we will have an excuse to act on our negative emotions in whatever form we desire. No! Remember that our aim is to be as emotionally oriented as we can and naturally that cannot involve actions like going on eating binges, watching TV all day, object-throwing, head-banging, wall-punching, masturbating, drinking, excessive screaming or cursing or exercising any other form of self-destructive behavior. (If you see where you have any of these tendencies, it is imperative that you address the problem immediately.) Instead, we should find intelligent, modest and healthy ways of yielding to and thus working through these negative emotions when they come.

So what are some intelligent, modest and healthy ways to vent our hurt, anger or frustration? Here are a few.

1. Exercise -- put on some disco music and get yourself moving.

2. Write a letter -- this should be directed toward the source or cause of your negative feeling. Just express all your thoughts and feelings as explicitly as you wish without holding back anything. When you're through, burn the letter.

3. Perform a chore -- clean the house, bathe the dog, wash the car, or do whatever needs to be done around the house.

4. Talk to someone -- choose someone you know and trust to talk to about what happened and about how you are feeling. Someone who is usually empathetic and warm. However, avoid seeking comfort from even a well-intentioned member of the opposite sex to whom you are not married. Dangerous things can happen.

5. Take a walk -- you can also take a long drive, but only if you are not too distraught.

6. Go shopping -- buy yourself something nice. It doesn't have to be expensive; just something cute or interesting or even just a surprise gift for a friend.

7 Take a nap -- lay down until you fall asleep, but before you do, tell yourself *convincingly* that upon awakening from your nap, you expect to be better.

8 Read -- find something motivating, humorous, soothing or encouraging to read.

9 My personal favorite -- just sit back in a comfortable chair and indulge yourself in the sounds of very lively classical music.

10 Cry -- cry as long and as hard as your soul desires. But, before you break down, put on some soft soothing music that may give you an even better cry. Then, tell yourself that the end of the music will signify the end of your weeping and thus your present distress. After which, you may choose to consummate your healing by taking a nice long nap. Doing these simple things may prevent you from feeling sorry for yourself and from crying yourself aimlessly into deeper depression.

There are so many other healthy options for us to choose whenever we become emotionally strained; and for married persons specifically, I've heard there is one in particular that is very effective.

So, whenever that **STOP** sign refuses to go up, go ahead and put up a **YIELD** sign and then proceed with care. But here's a reminder: don't forget to *take down* that yield sign at the end of it all. ☺

Exercise Reasonableness

Near the beginning of this chapter, a brief profile of an emotionally oriented person was given. If you remember, it was said that such a person is not immune to annoyances, irritations, disappointments or feelings of deep concern. This is important for us to accept and to remember whenever we experience any of these. We need to remember that we are not perfect and so experiencing such feelings do not mean that we are emotionally disoriented. It is when we regularly encourage them and act on them that we become emotionally disoriented.

Develop Your Own Personal Strategy

By use of your imagination and creative innovation, you can develop your own personal strategy for keeping yourself emotionally controlled. While it is good to learn already established methods of emotional orientation, it is always best for you to create your own method, one that is uniquely from you. Even if you modify other known methods, the result will still be one unique to you.

Creating your own method will serve to sharpen your ability to reason and to discern for yourself the areas in your tendencies that need improvement or adjustment. Consequently, you will be better able to cut your own path toward emotional orientation. Furthermore, no other human can know you better than you can know yourself and so more than likely, the method you devise for yourself will be most compatible with your personal capabilities. In other words; when all the ideas of the world have flown, for you one shall remain, since to each is his own.

Final Remarks

For most of us, attaining emotional orientation will mean facing up to many serious challenges and making many personal sacrifices. After all, we are living in a very imperfect world made up of very imperfect people, ourselves included. However, with earnest efforts and constant awareness and determination, this seemingly sophisticated art of emotional orientation can be mastered, at least to the degree possible for any imperfect human being.

There are so many wonderful blessings that you can create for yourself when you develop emotional orientation. Blessings of enduring love, joy, lasting friendships, good health, power and peace. You will be giving yourself the gift of truly living, since unlike in the case of an emotionally disoriented person, those around you will come to know and love your worthwhile qualities and attributes instead of anticipating and avoiding unwelcomed displays of negative emotions.

As for intense, prolonged emotional trials. Your consistent practice with cultivating emotional orientation even in the trivial situations in your life, will build you up and advance your ability to persevere and to endure these when they come along.

I want us to now take a look at one particular emotion that I believe deserves exclusive consideration. Fear.

Chapter Three

Fear

Nothing in life is to be feared,
it is only to be understood.

Marie Curie

Anxiety, apprehension, terror, panic, phobia. All these words describe the painful emotion called fear. It is an emotion we all feel occasionally and is excited by a sense of impending danger or dread. There are basically two types of fear that affect our lives. Natural fears: the fear of fire, fear of being raped or violently attacked, fear of a chronic disease, fear of danger, fear of death and so on. Then there are neurotic fears. These are the fears that are created by our own inner thoughts and our own fearful expectations. Neurotic fears live only inside our heads and are fed purely by the fallacious perceptions we form throughout life. These fears immobilize us on the road to self-improvement because they hinder us from taking the challenging steps necessary to do so. It is not until we get rid of them or at least learn to keep them under control that we will be able to make better use of our potential. In this chapter, we will discuss just a few of these neurotic fears along with suggestions for dealing with them.

Confront It Head On

I'm sure you've probably heard it said that the only way to overcome any fear is to confront it head on. This is true. Courage enough to challenge our fears is the platinum key to conquering them. Now, because neurotic fears are formed within our minds, it is there that we must go in order to meet them and so deal with them. We must go inside our minds and first identify what our fears are; the fears we have unwittingly taught ourselves throughout life. Then, after patient and keen analysis, unteach ourselves these fears and see them for what they are -- neurotic. Our level of experience with confronting our fears is what will determine the degree of success we will have with overcoming them. That experience comes from the developed ability to determine the roots of our fears and from understanding the tendencies we have that may contribute to them. Let us now look at a few examples of neurotic fears along with some platinum keys that can be used to overcome them.

CONFRONTING: The Fear of Failure

It is the fear of failure that may explain the butterflies in our stomachs whenever we are preparing for a job interview, an examination, to take on an important task, to participate in a competition et cetera. We become anxious, nervous and we begin anticipating the worst. The erroneous reasoning that nurtures this fear is that: this *task (that we might fail at) is a test of our individual competence and ability to succeed; so if we fail, then we obviously are not good enough or capable enough of succeeding.* Then we may go on asking ourselves (sometimes subconsciously), questions like: if I fail at this task, what kind of person will I really be proving myself to be? If I fail at doing *this* then how will I possibly be able to do *that*? Paul, Jane and Bob must be better than I since they didn't fail at it, what will they think of me if *I* fail? What will my parents and everyone else I know think of me? After all they *are* expecting me to succeed. How will I explain my failure to them? Does any of this sound familiar to you? Not to worry. There are simple remedies for this common problem. Let's take a look at a few.

1 In any given situation, first ask yourself: what's the worst that could happen? For example, let's say you are playing a match in a tennis tournament. The worst possible thing that could happen is that you could fail to win the match right? Now, let us say this does indeed happen and as they say, you 'lost' the match. Think about it, did you really *lose* anything? Well let's see. Your ability to play tennis is still there. Your previous successes in tennis matches will always still be there. Your love for the game, hopefully, will still be there. So, what it really boils down to is this: the worst that could possibly happen is that you will be in the exact position as you were before the game. You can't be any worse

off, only perhaps a little better because you will have gained more experience in playing the game.

2 Recognize and accept that not because you failed at something *today* means that you will fail at it again in the future. As time goes by you will gain more experience, more confidence and hence more competence for your next attempt.

3 Prepare as best as you can for the task at hand. Think carefully of anything at all that you can do to give yourself as much of an advantage in meeting the challenge as possible and do those things.

4 Avoid comparing yourself with your peers, remembering that their circumstances, strengths and abilities are different from yours and so naturally their pattern of successes and failures will too be different from yours.

5 Whenever you have personal plans for tasks or challenges you wish to take on, avoid getting into too much detail about them with everyone who asks of them. Contain your excitement and anticipation and share your plans only with a close select few. This way you will avoid the burden of having to explain and re-explain the possible unfavorable outcomes of your personal efforts to persons who no doubt will ask of them. It can only hurt your self-confidence to have to remind yourself

continuously of your failed task, which is just what you will be doing in these unnecessary and avoidable explanations.

6 Before your attempt to accomplish any mission, remind yourself of your previous successes in accomplishing other goals. Re-identify yourself with your achieved successes and feel all over again all the positive emotions that went along with those successes. Doing this will not only build up your confidence and courage to face the fresh challenge, but these positive reminders will also serve as comfort and reassurance to you should you fail at the upcoming task. Since then, you could honestly and easily say to yourself: "Well, I wasn't quite successful this time around, but look at all the other times I was? I have good skills and abilities, not to mention tremendous potential, my previous accomplishments reflect evidence of that. I know I can't win them all so perhaps next time will be my turn again."

7 Before taking on any task, ask yourself this question: "When I turn eighty, will the outcome of this task *really* matter?" 9½ out of 10 the answer will be 'no.'

CONFRONTING:
The Fear of Difficult Situations

The primary cause for the fear of difficult situations is insecurity. A person faced with a difficult situation may doubt his own ability to handle it in a way that will yield a favorable result. This automatically threatens his peace of mind, his comfort zone and so arouses in him fear and anxiety. He may then want to do one of two things. Either rely on someone else to shoulder his problem for him, assuming that that person is better able to do so, or, in an effort to quickly rid himself of the problem, impatiently make rash steps without asking for help or thinking rationally through the issue. Both these choices should be avoided. Some wiser choices for him would be to:

1. Try as best to keep calm and to control his emotions. That way he will be better able to think more rationally and logically instead of responding emotionally or foolishly.

2. He should try to appreciate that it is only by working through difficult situations that he can gain experience and grow to maturity. This way he will appreciate the challenge, deeming it as another opportunity toward further advancement.

3. He should try to examine the situation as keenly as possible, looking at it in its entirety. Perhaps he may want to write down all the components of the

situation and determine which ones are real and which are imaginary; which ones are changeable and which are not; which ones he can work out on his own and which ones he may need assistance for. That way he can organize his best plan of action.

4 He should seek the necessary help he needs from more experienced persons than himself. This will contribute to helping him make the best possible decisions and to develop the confidence and the courage to act as wisely as he can in dealing with his difficult situation.

Yes, if we practice this approach to dealing with difficult situations, our fear of them, as we gain more experience, will gradually turn into excitement by their challenges.

CONFRONTING:
The Fear of Dealing with 'Important' People

Like all other fears, confronting this one in order to conquer it requires experience. Fortunately one can begin working on this right away because as long as there are people there are opportunities to deal with them.

In this world a person is thought of as being powerful or important if he is wealthy, popular, good looking, highly intellectual, academically accomplished or talented. If you are one of those persons who attaches importance to any of the above mentioned descriptions, then your first step to overcoming the fear of dealing with such persons is to rid yourself completely of that idea. Do not be fooled by the illusion that such persons are powerful or important just because *other people* look up to them, giving them titles and singing their praises. They only become powerful or important to you when *you* view them that way -- not because they are. Here are a few keys we can use to successfully deal with 'important' people.

1 Make conscious efforts to look persons directly in their eyes when speaking with them. Do not evade their stare by glancing away, looking down, or pretending to be preoccupied with something else. A tip on how you can successfully master this is to, in the back of your mind, pretend that there is a tiny purple blotch somewhere in the person's eyes and that it is important that you look hard and long enough to see it. Of course, you should remember that this blotch is only imaginary and so you need to keep your mind focused on your dealings with this person and not on the non-existent blotch.

2 Address persons bearing titles such as Doctor, Professor, Sir and so on by their first names. As long as you are an adult you have absolutely no reason to be afraid of doing so. This is not to say that there is anything negative about using these titles when necessary, but just knowing that you are confident enough to call, say, your doctor 'Bill' rather than

'Dr. Johnson' *at least once if you wanted to* will in itself help you to put your fear of dealing with him in perspective.

3 If you become nervous when speaking to someone, make yourself aware of it and avoid giving in to it. Also, avoid stuttering, rambling on or displaying any form of out-of-control behavior. Speak slowly and deliberately if you need to, thinking on *what you are saying* and not on *how you are appearing* to the one listening to you.

Fear strangles Self-Improvement

4 Maintain a pleasant disposition and a good sense of humor. Try to reflect your true personality rather than an unnaturally formal or a defensive one.

Insight On Dealing with the Feeling of Intimidation

Can you think of someone who makes you feel intimidated? Who makes you feel nervous, insecure, or as if you are in some way lacking? Perhaps you can because this is not unusual. In fact all of us at one point in time experience intimidation and will agree that it is a very unpleasant and stressful feeling.

So, is there any way you can approach this problem and successfully deal with it? Sure. Think again of this person who usually intimidates you. Now ask yourself: Is there a specific quality about this person that I find appealing or consider to be special? Is there something outstanding that he (or she) has accomplished that deeply impresses me? Do the quality or quantity of his possessions make mine seem inferior? Is my perception of him influenced in any way by other people's perception of him?

Asking yourself questions like these will help you to see clearly what exactly it is about this person that arouses intimidation in you. In most cases, you will find that it is not really the ***person himself*** *that causes the intimidation, but* *it is a subconscious perception of him that in some way reflects a personal desire or lacking in you. There is something about this person that you perceive as being either powerful or fascinating and this thing, though you desire it, is not something you think you have. To further explain: Let's say you feel intimidated by someone intellectual, physically beautiful or intriguing. The only reason you can possibly have for feeling this way is if you are in some way drawn to this person but subconsciously you do not consider yourself to be intellectual, physically beautiful or intriguing enough. It is as simple as that. You cannot be intimidated by something familiar to you, something you already possess or are used to experiencing. The rich do not intimidate the rich – they intimidate the poor. The intellectual do not intimidate the intellectual – they intimidate the unintellectual. The rough do not intimidate the rough – they intimidate the gentle. Do you see the point?*

Now, once you can identify what exactly it is that causes your intimidation, you are well on your way to overcoming or at least controlling it. The trick now is to disassociate this intimidating quality or characteristic from the persons that display it and focus only on this cause and it's effect on you. It is important that you be completely honest and candid with yourself when discerning the reason for your intimidation; then you will be able to make genuine progress.

So, now you have figured out what the cause is. What next? Well, here are a few suggestions.

1 *Do not avoid the person/s displaying the intimidating quality, nor should you go out of your way to get their attention or to get them to accept you. Doing any of these things will only serve to feed your subconscious mind with the erroneous idea that these persons are above you in some way, and this in itself will only compound your feeling of intimidation.*

2 *If the intimidating quality or characteristic is something that would logically be beneficial to you and it is something that you can right now work on developing, try in your own way to do so. For instance, if the quality is something like self-confidence, brightness or physical fitness or attractiveness, perhaps you may want to give a little extra attention to these areas. Be practical and balanced but patient and consistent in your efforts.*

3 *If the intimidating quality or characteristic is something like wealth, popularity, height, the acquisition of a prestigious degree, skin or eye color, or anything of this sort, you need to be realistic in your reasoning. You can always try to get these things but my guess is that you'll probably only end up hurting yourself. Not to say that it is impossible to obtain say wealth or a Ph.D, but it cannot be healthy to strive for these things on the premise that you are inadequate without*

them. As for height and skin color, you cannot change these things so you will need only to accept them, and what is more, learn to love them.

What you will need to do when dealing with unattainable qualities or characteristics that intimidate you, is to adjust your perception of them. While you might still admire them (unlike the fox and the 'sour' grapes), you need to view them differently than you do now. You need to find a psychological way of attaching less importance or significance to them.

4 *Recognize that not because some quality or characteristic intimidates you, means that it is something worth having. For instance, prominence, aggressiveness, excessive wealth, or even the ability to control or manipulate others are things that you may find intimidating – but not things that are necessarily beneficial or healthy.*

5 *If all else fails, imagine the person/s displaying the intimidating characteristics, as not having them. Suppose Mr. Pee-aych-dee's circumstances in life led him instead to be a bus boy? Suppose that gorgeous person you know, met in a terrible accident and became disfigured? Suppose Mr. Popular, who no one can seem to live without, was left stranded alone on a deserted island forever? Reasoning on questions like these will help you to*

see that these people are only human. Really, what would they be like if they did not have these seemingly admirable attributes? What would they be like inside? Would they still intimidate you? Would they have attractive qualities that would make you still want to be like them? Think about that. You may just start viewing them more realistically and seeing that these qualities or characteristics that they display – that you find intimidating – are really just superficial or overrated.

CONFRONTING:
The Fear of Being One's Self

As the well known saying goes: 'All the world's a stage.' It is the seemingly normal thing for people to put on facade. They do this in order to create impressions that are deemed favorable or admirable to the world -- their audience. People who fall victim to this self-defeating tendency become afraid of being themselves. They cannot be certain of the kind of reception they will receive and so in their minds, if they should be themselves, they risk being disfavored by those around them. They pretend and pretend they're not pretending. They live inside themselves and remain trapped in their own hidden world in which they alone are their own audience. Chances are, you are one of such persons. If you suspect that you are, not to worry. Here are a few suggestions to help you to effectively confront this fear.

1. Without comparing yourself with anyone else, think of all the interesting, unique qualities about yourself that you know are admirable and positive. They may include a talent, a skill, a delightful sense of humor, anything. Write them down and appreciate and enjoy them first *with yourself.*

2. Expand and improve on them if you think you can or need to.

3. Share those positive aspects of yourself first with people who you already feel close to. *Do not choose someone whose approval you feel you must get.* First, practice expressing your uniqueness to the ones who right now really matter. The ones who will accept you unconditionally like your family members and closest friends. This will help you to witness first hand the effects of your unique, positive qualities on other people and cause you to love and appreciate your *true* self even more. Consequently, you will become more confident in expressing your true self and will eventually find it easier to do so at all times.

4. Avoid the regular company of pretenders, people who are constantly seeking to be accepted, or persons who decide to be anti-social because they

fear being themselves. Instead, stick with persons who love their true selves and who aren't afraid of expressing it.

5 Show appreciation for others' unique characteristics. This will encourage them to be *their* true selves and help you to gain their then worthwhile friendships. Remember, if you put down others or negatively criticize them for some unique or unusual characteristic of theirs, you will, without even realizing it, be creating in your own subconscious mind, the erroneous and burdensome issue of what 'acceptable' characteristics are. This will only sink you deeper into the quicksand of the fear of being your true self.

CONFRONTING:
The Fear of Never Connecting Intimately with Another Human Being

As humans, all of us have the desire to intimately connect with each other. We all want to know that there is at least one other person who we can honestly communicate our feelings to, share our deepest thoughts with and be our truest selves around. Unfortunately, in this world, identifying such a person can be very difficult. Difficult because perhaps we may not have yet encountered someone with a similar thinking pattern, or with similar interests as ours, in order to identify with and appreciate us.

Or, it may be difficult because of what we might have allowed ourselves to become as a result of this lacking in our lives. We may end up being one of two kinds of persons.

We may, out of desperation, be the sort to give too much of ourselves to another person too soon. This kind of person tends to trust too easily and expects the same right away from the person whose friendship he pursues. When his prospective best friend, perhaps now turned off by or suspicious of him, does not respond in the way he hoped, he ends up feeling hurt, embarrassed and frustrated. This then leads to him being the second kind of person. After being tired of being rebuffed, he may permanently recoil. He may isolate himself from the persons he knows and become selfish, overly suspicious of the innocent intentions of others, bitter, spiteful, or obnoxious.

If you suspect that you may be at least, on your way to becoming like any of these persons, here are a few suggestions.

1. Obtain a journal and convey all your personal thoughts and feelings in writing. This way you can refer to it at a future time with a view to understanding yourself more intimately.

2. If you are an animal lover -- get a pet. I know that pets cannot substitute for humans but you will be

surprised at what their friendships can help you to understand about yourself.

3 Share a little of yourself at a time with others and spread yourself around instead of zeroing in on some 'ideal' person. Before you know it, your special friends will become evident in your life.

4 Reach out to others instead of waiting for others to reach out to you.

5 Be as much of your true self as possible when relating to others. Remember, when it comes to friendships, the only ones that count are the ones who accept you for who you really are.

6 Be patient, and while you wait, continue to seek ways to grow as a person, getting to know yourself better, so that you will have a lot more to offer to your friendships when they do come.

CONFRONTING: The Fear of Loss

The fear of loss is primarily based on the premise that the event of losing something significant automatically depreciates the value of self. The idea is that: My life (me) is made up of 'x', 'y' and 'z' and if I lose 'z', then my life is just 'x' and 'y' and so it is of less value than it was before. Because of this, people will, when they have experienced a loss, try at all costs to replace what they lost as soon as possible. That way, they can begin again to feel whole, complete and of significant value.

So now, how do we go about confronting this fear of loss and successfully control it? Well, here is a practical method that works for me. All you will need is paper, a pen, about 20 minutes and a bit of insightful information.

Now, here is that bit of insightful information: whenever you are confronted with the fear of losing something, recognize that it is not *that thing* per se that you dread losing the most. What you really fear losing are the *accompanying benefits that you subconsciously associate with that particular thing.*

Now here is what you will do with the pen and paper.

i) Write down a list of the main things in your life that you fear losing.

ii) Beside each one, write down what you think are the advantages, benefits or joys of having them. (These are the things that you have subconsciously associated with your precious possessions)

iii) On a separate piece of paper, write down your most commonly stated advantages, benefits and joys. (These will actually be the things you value the *most* and that you fear losing most.

After you have identified what these most valuable assets are, your final step is to learn how to nurture and improve on anything that is associated with those personal assets. In most cases, these have little to do with the elements you likely wrote in Step one. Here is a simple example. This is Mindy Lawson's list.

* STEP ONE — * STEP TWO

My job – control, security, a purpose/meaning, stimulation

My health – joy, life, control, security, capability, peace of mind

My husband – security, love, joy, companionship, a purpose/meaning

My material possesions – joy, security, control, capability, peace of mind

My friendships – love, companionship, joy, security, a purpose/meaning

My youth – control, independence, health, peace of mind, capability

* STEP THREE

Security, Control, Joy, Peace of mind, Capability, a Purpose/Meaning

So by this practical exercise, Mindy Lawson is able to derive the things that mean the most to her and what she always desires to have (step 3). As you can see, these things are not the things that she has a conscious fear of losing (step 1); they are only *the means* by which she feels she can obtain these things (by means of her job, her health, her husband and so on).

So what Mindy now needs to do is to become more aware of the things that really mean the most to her; control of her life, peace of mind, security, joy, capability, and a purpose or meaning. And then, in a healthy, balanced way, seek to find many *different* ways and means of maintaining those things. She needs to be creative in finding these different ways so that she will be less likely to depend solely on her job, health, husband and so on to satisfy her true needs and desires.

Automatically, her fear of losing these things will be put under control since there will be other aspects of her life that will be stimulating her deepest and truest needs. As her fear of losing her job, health, husband etc dissipates, she will even begin to find more pleasure in them, since then, she will be better able to enjoy the experiences they bring, rather than concentrating on just *keeping* them. She may find that her performance on the job will improve since she will subconsciously be less tense about it. Consequently, her health will also improve and she will become more balanced in her efforts to maintain it. She may find that her relationship with her husband becomes less superficial; her view of material possessions more modest; her friendships richer, and the thought of growing old may never again be a concern of hers.

However long this little exercise may take, if done honestly and meaningfully, it will help you significantly to confront and control your fear of loss.

CONFRONTING: The Fear of Fear

'There is nothing to fear but fear itself' so the popular saying goes. But this gives rise to the question: If fear is to be feared, how then must we rid ourselves of it? Simply, we cannot. If we again look at Marie Curie's words *nothing in life is to be feared, it is only to be understood*, it is quite reasonable to conclude that this principle should apply also to '*fear itself*'. Yes, fear is not to be feared, it is only to be understood.

With the proper understanding of fear comes the reassurance that it is not some powerful, active force out to overcome us. It is simply a state of mind created by a concept or a perception or combinations of such. These concepts and perceptions are totally controllable since they are created within our own minds and are lifeless and changeable.

So how can we control even overcome the fear of fear? Here are a few tips we can use.

1 Whenever you are about to be faced with a potentially fearsome experience, try not to *anticipate* the fear. You can do this by avoiding fearsome imaginations of the experience. In other words, if

it is an inevitable one, allow the experience to come to you rather than you prematurely 'going' to it.

2 Undermine fear by pretending that it is not at all a part of you but instead is some foreign emotion that occasionally and briefly passes through you.

3 Before facing your potentially fearsome experience, calmly admit to yourself that you are aware that this experience is one that may, logically thinking, give rise to a feeling of fear. But then after bringing to the surface this admission, immediately downplay it by choosing to take an 'illogical' or 'abnormal' approach -- that of *defying* the expected fear.

4 If all else fails, take a good long look again at 'Mr. Fear', then ask yourself: Should *I* be afraid of *him* or should *he* be afraid of *me*? By the looks of this character or even by his name alone, the answer should be clear to you. ☺

In Closing

There are so many more neurotic fears that we could discuss together. Cancers of the mind we have nurtured inside us perhaps for a long time and that left untreated continue to grow. Poisons that immobilize us and slowly suffocate our prospects for self- advancement. A few more common examples are: fear of **the unknown**, fear of

commitment, the fear of **change,** the fear of **hard work**, of **being alone**, or of **responsibility.** The fear of **intimacy**, of **being poor**, the fear of **making mistakes** or of **facing the truth**.

As mentioned before, it is only experience in confronting such destructive fears that will help us to eliminate them; and once we have the *awareness* of each of them and are able to identify *their roots*, we can be confident that we have the necessary tools with which to gain that experience. Make it a habit of yours, whenever you become aware of a personal fear, to spend a little time to candidly analyze it. After you have come to even a basic understanding of it, jot down tactics that *you* think will be effective in overcoming it. Don't make a big deal of it though by laboring over it for hours, this might only serve to complicate and intensify the fear. Just act promptly, decisively and above all -- boldly, with a view to resolving or at least controlling it as best as possible. As the famous German poet Johann von Goethe once said:

> *"What you can, or dream you can,* ***begin it****;*
> ***Boldness*** *has genius, power and magic in it."*

So begin now my friend and be on your way to a bold new you.

Speaking of 'beginning now', let us next look at something that often prevents us from doing so.

Chapter Four

That Wretched Force Called Inertia

An object continues in a state of rest -- or in a state of motion at a constant speed -- along a straight line -- unless compelled to change that state by a net force.

Isaac Newton's Law of Inertia

The Law of Inertia of course refers to masses relative to their physical motion. However, the law can be applied to our minds relative to our psychological, sociological, emotional and mental motions as well. I'll just substitute a few expressions in Newton's law to support this claim: A *person continues in a state of apathy -- or in a state of existence at a constant level -- in one dimension -- unless compelled to change that state by motivated effort.* This is the Law of Inertia as it relates to our minds.

Inertia is a potent force that exists in different degrees in all of us. It is the natural tendency to want to remain undisturbed or in a constant state within a comfort zone.

Inertia is what causes procrastination and hence the wasting of much precious time and potential. It subtly but effectively oppresses our true potential by fooling us

Mr. Inertia

sometimes into believing that we are already doing all that we are capable of. Inertia left unchallenged results in laziness that lulls us into a stupor of non-progressiveness. When this happens, we may tend to begin finding all sorts of excuses for our failure to achieve; perhaps blaming it on life, our families, our bosses, our teachers, the system, our health, our childhood, the weather or just about anything we can. This generates even more support for our state of apathy, feeding and strengthening the force of inertia and so making it even more difficult to get into motion so to speak.

As was alluded to earlier, we need to challenge inertia if we expect to overcome it and so make progress. But how? Pay close attention to this illustration highlighting some simple, natural laws of physics, which will reveal the proper approach needed to do so.

Let us say there is a heavy brick lying on a surface. It has been lying there for a reasonably long time. The brick is able to lie there instead of moving, for as long as it has because of the static frictional forces parallel to the surface acting on it. Now, what about if you tried to move the brick? Well, if the force used is small, the brick will not move because the static frictional force exactly cancels the effect of the applied force. If you should increase the applied force by a small amount, the brick will still remain in a state of rest. This is because the static frictional force *also increases* by an amount that cancels out the increase made of the applied force. However, *if the applied force continues to increase*, there will come a point when the brick will finally 'break away' and slide. After that point, the applied force needed to keep the brick moving will be less than the initial applied force and so it will be easier to keep the brick moving from then on.

How does this apply to our discussion? Well, if you are a victim of inertia, the brick in this case could represent your inner potential. It has been lying within you for a while. It lies there instead of accomplishing anything because of laziness and failure to make positive efforts. Now, what about if you tried to make use of your potential? Well, if the effort you put out is small, your potential will not convert into accomplishment. This is because the months or years of accumulated apathy, which may have developed into laziness, along with the mastered ability to find excuses, or to blame others for your non-progressiveness, will find a way to exactly cancel the effect of your applied effort. If you

Inertia enjoys sitting on Your Potential

should increase your effort by a small amount, your potential will still remain dormant. This is because the inertia will also increase to resist and cancel out your increased effort. This is why it may sometimes appear that you are not capable of succeeding since every time you attempt to do something positive, something else makes it harder for you. But do not be fooled. If your applied effort *continues to increase* there *will* come a point when your potential will finally 'break away' and be converted into accomplishment. After that point, the applied effort needed to keep utilizing your potential will be less than the initial 'break away' effort you made and so it will be easier for you to keep on converting your potential into success from then on.

Fear feeds Inertia and makes him grow.

Why did I choose to use this seemingly far-fetched, scientific illustration? Well, to help you to see that the 'problem' of inertia is a scientific one and hence in any form it can be treated logically and practically. From this illustration, we have seen clearly that by the laws of *science*, (not just by the laws of society or common sense), intense initial effort is needed before we can get the ball rolling, the brick sliding or the potential converting.

Now, let us look at some platinum keys to applying this needed effort.

1. Make an outline of your daily routine on paper. Change it completely by omitting the areas that waste your time. For instance, watching excessive television, spending long hours on the phone, daydreaming or surfing the Net. Understandably, it would be unreasonable for you to try to overnightly cease from all your regular idle activities. What you can do though, is to set a limit or a prescribed quota for the time spent on each of them. As time goes by, keep cutting the time down until your system will no longer be programmed to automatically perform those idle activities. Also, omit the areas that you deem to in any way hinder your efforts to break free from inertia, as well as areas that may increase your dependency on anyone or anything.

2. Recognize that fear, as discussed in the previous chapter, feeds inertia and makes it greater. So make the effort to control as many of your fears as you can. This will enable you to more confidently face the challenges that will no doubt be presented to you.

3. Set reasonable goals for yourself and meditate on your approach to attaining them.

4 Imagine yourself already being successful at achieving your goals. Pretend as though you have never at any time been a lazy person, but that you have always been hardworking and are very familiar with accomplishment. This will help to turn your mind on to a more positive and advanced frequency.

5 Instead of thinking of the drastic changes you will have to make all at once, concentrate on your efforts to change **one day at a time**. If you wish, you can even fool that lazy side of yourself by pretending that you will be working hard for *just that* day. Of course, if you are going to use this tactic, be sure to use it *every day*.

6 When you have got the hang of accomplishing more of your goals, be careful that you do not become too excited and begin setting for yourself too many or unrealistic goals. Reason being; if you should fail to accomplish them all, that failure can give rise to a false sense of inadequacy which can plunge you right back into apathy. This will make it even more difficult for you to get started again because you might feel that your hard efforts were and will always be in vain. You may then lose confidence in yourself and develop a fear of failure, further compounding your problem.

7 Very importantly -- ask for help. Confide in someone that you trust who does not himself suffer from inertia. Confess your problem to him and inform him of your strategy to improve yourself, while you remain open to any suggestions he might make. You will find this very supporting and encouraging. Bear in mind that if you happen not to know well anyone like this, you can choose a partner who suffers from inertia *but* who is as determined or even more determined to overcome the problem as you are.

Final Remarks

If you can think of other methods that you can employ to overcome this wretched problem of inertia, by all means make the best of them. Muster up the courage and the determination needed to approach all your efforts. Work hard. I guarantee you, your efforts will not be in vain. Be patient and reasonable with yourself and maintain diligence. Before you know it, your life will be filled with excitement and fulfillment as your potential will continue to grow and to convert into personal success. Congratulations in advance.

Chapter Five

Fallacious Perception

A man's perception becomes his own reality,
Although reality by him is not always perceived,
Herein lies the exquisite tragedy,
Of a man, who himself continues to deceive.

SAS

Perception, according to author Philip Cotler, may be defined as "the process by which an individual selects, organizes and interprets information inputs to create a meaningful picture of the world." A fallacy may be defined as a 'false idea', 'erroneous reasoning', 'something misleading', 'illogical' or 'deceptive.' Hence, we can define fallacious perception as *an illogical process by which a misled individual selects, organizes, and interprets information inputs to create an erroneous picture of the world.* Sounds messy doesn't it? Yes it does. Fallacious perceptions are messy and they will mess with your mind. They come in all shapes, sizes and forms and are almost always carefully disguised. They present themselves in most of life's situations and it is not until we become aware that they exist that we will be able to prevent them from becoming a part of our thinking.

Mr. Fallacious Perception

A person who thinks based on fallacious perception, unwittingly incurs ongoing victimization. This is because in a world of reality, he lives unreality. In a world of color, he lives black and white. In a world of truth, he lives a lie.

Fallacious perceivers, without realizing it, make several poor choices and unnecessary mistakes in their lives. For them, the consequences of these mistakes are always painful, sometimes tragic, but to them such consequences are merely unavoidable misfortunes. It is almost as if they are constantly building a house without knowing that it has not got a foundation and so end up spending the rest of their lives constantly repairing damages, sometimes having to rebuild after a collapse. In other words, they fail to interpret life's situations accurately and are constantly paying the price.

The ability to accurately perceive and understand life's situations is based on learned awareness. A person attaining this kind of awareness does so by continuously seeking insight, which he gains from his acquired knowledge and experience. Unlike a fallacious perceiver, he constantly seeks to find the *truth* behind a matter, examining situations in their lengths, breadths, and depths. He is always discerning, discriminating, and aware of the basis for his reasoning on any matter or situation. An accurate perceiver may ask himself questions like: This problem that's nagging me, is it a real problem or is it just imaginary? Is this view of mine logical, rational, or is it purely emotional or bias? Is the person that offended me really a horrible person who I should dislike or avoid ~ or pity? After all, instead of being a downright horrible person, he could just be one of the many emotionally dysfunctional persons battling with internal conflicts or personal problems that manifest themselves in his behavior. He may also ask himself questions like: Is my general mode of thinking and the firm beliefs I hold, whether moral, religious, social or otherwise, based on sound reasoning? Or are they based on tradition, prejudices, the influences of my environment or on natural tendencies? (For instance: to want to do what's easiest or to not want to be considered as odd). Answers to these and other similar questions help a person to effectively discern or 'size-up', a situation and so perceive it in a more accurate way.

Perception may be learned from what we have grown up seeing and hearing. But while we learn what we live, we do not always have to live what we learn. If the persons we grew up with, including our own parents, are themselves fallacious perceivers, it does not stand to reason that we ourselves must be likewise. Each of us, at some stage in our life must take responsibility for our own perceptive ability. This is done by independently aspiring to gain further insight on life's situations, with a view to bringing one's self to an advanced standard of being. That of being psychologically emancipated and emotionally unoppressed. In many cases, this can be very difficult since it will call for the rooting out of many fallacious perceptions learned throughout our entire lives. And, on top of that, making the needed effort can sometimes result in the disfavor of others, unfortunately, even loved ones.

Let us now discuss and analyze just three examples of fallacious perceptions. Doing this will serve to guide us in our approach to dealing with any other fallacious perception we may hold in our minds.

Fallacious Perception # 1: *"If I don't do what everyone else is doing, even if it is wrong, then I won't be accepted by others and if I am not accepted by others then I can never be truly happy."*

This is a very common perception held by millions of persons today. Chances are, you may be one of them. Because of a lack of self-worth and low self-esteem, such persons find it easier to place confidence in the beliefs and opinions of others rather than those of themselves, deeming everyone else, sometimes even without realizing it, as superior. By doing so, they commit the folly of regarding everyone they know with great importance. If you are such a person, it is urgent that you teach yourself to define just who is and who isn't really important to you. To do so, you can ask yourself questions like: 'To what extent is this person a part of my life? What level of obligation do I rightly have *not feel* toward him? Just how much good does this person really mean for me?' Honest answers to such questions may reveal that the person on which you placed so much importance is really not that important after all, maybe not even necessary to your life.

"But," you may ask, "what if I am rejected by someone I consider to be important?" Well, it all boils back down to the amount of value you place on yourself. Just how high and how readily do you esteem and consult *your own* standards as the authority for choosing your personal contentment? Do you even have such personal standards for yourself? Do you know what they are? Or have you chosen the easiest path most taken ~ that of allowing others to define for you your personal standards for choosing happiness? If that is the case, you need to recognize that such a decision is a tragic blunder on your part. No other human being should you allow to choose the standards or criteria for your feeling accepted and contented. *It is only when you deem other persons' standards as the authority for personal acceptance that the pain of rejection can be experienced.*

Insight on Rejection

Please be aware that there is a lot more to a person's acceptance or rejection of others than meets the eye. It is not always a matter of whether someone likes or dislikes another person for him to determine whether he'll accept or reject him. In fact, in many cases, likes and dislikes have nothing at all to do with the deciding process. Sadly, one of the things that some people commonly do in order to feel important is to shun others or put them down. By doing so they seek to convey to themselves the idea that, somehow, they are superior to the one they shun. They feel a deep need to assert their own feeling of self-importance and since the whole idea is to rank themselves among other people, rejecting others (seemingly for no apparent reason) is often the method used. Bear in mind however that they too have their own 'superior' person who puts them down occasionally. Maybe a boss, a wealthy associate, a bossy husband or wife or a higher achiever. It's sort of like a hierarchy of rejecters in which they fit somewhere. Their aim however is to have as many people in their downline as possible; that way, they heighten their position on this illusionary pyramid of rejecters.

Of course, there is another way to look at it. Persons may appear to reject others if for some reason they are intimidated by them. They may pretend to dislike a person and concoct all sorts of erroneous reasons for not accepting him, when the truth is simply that they are afraid to have to relate to the person. This person may be brighter than they are, better looking, wealthier, or simply happier or more confident. And so, this poses a threat to their 'applecart' so to speak, their comfort zone, their own sense of self-security and self-worth. So what better way for them to try to feel more important than to feign rejection? Doing so in the hopes of intimidating the one who secretly intimidates them. These sorts of people gravitate toward each other and tend to band together in cliques, clubs, gangs, and fraternities – anything that can possibly create an impression of exclusiveness or an aura of superiority. Whenever their feigning rejection tactic fails and that one ignores these would-be victimizers, they feel beaten at their own game. As a result, they may collectively become cruel. They may mock or tease their subject; create false stories and rumors and relentlessly gossip about the person, hoping to get his attention by hurting his feelings and hence controlling him. Or, individually they may become humbled and even more impressed or fascinated by this person and therefore, quit the charade.

The final word on this matter is, that if you are not obnoxious, considered a bad influence, a criminal, dirty, smelly or possess any other quality that may obviously be found repulsive, then someone's rejection of you is completely unwarranted. In most cases it simply means that he (or she) is, in some way, battling with his own need to feel important and to be accepted by others. This problem is manifested in his being anti-social, snobby, insultive, obnoxious and so on. These persons are not all bad, so don't be angry with them or despise them. Just make sure that you do not fall victim to this sick but common trap and simply pity those who do.

Fallacious Perception #2: *Money and material gain is the panacea for human unhappiness.*

"Money can't buy happiness" is a well-known cliché. Perhaps it is one you yourself have used in times passed. One question that is worth considering though is, do you *really* believe that statement? Do you really believe that money and material gain; the capability to enjoy the finer things in life that only wealth can afford, will not bring you total happiness? If you think about it and answer yourself honestly, you may be surprised at what you come up with.

The truth is, most unwealthy persons and even some wealthy ones, believe that if they were richer, then somehow their happiness would be greater. This in itself is not an unreasonable thought, in fact, it is a very logical one. It stands to reason that if one is rich, then he is able to enjoy certain luxuries in life that will contribute to his total happiness. Also he can afford things that can enhance his health and so his physical and mental well-being can be maintained at a relatively high level.

So what is my point then? Am I not saying that money *can* buy happiness? Perhaps it sounds that way so let me now draw attention to the real fallacy in this reasoning. Yes, money can buy happiness -- but only a *very limited* amount. There does exist a point of diminishing returns, as there is only so much and no more that money can do. You see, with money, we can always avail ourselves of material things that can give us pleasure. Paradoxically however, pleasure in itself contributes little to our genuine happiness. How so? Pleasure is merely the result of positive stimulation of our senses whether it be sight, sound, smell, taste or sensation; all these things being *external.* On the other hand, true happiness is experienced only when a deep feeling of inner contentment resulting from a clean conscience, genuine self-love, heartfelt gratification and a sense of true purpose or meaning are regularly stimulated -- the root of these being *internal.* These attributes can mainly be obtained by living and sharing with our fellow human beings and other living creatures in Godly love and harmony. Happiness results when we are able to fully love and appreciate others and to allow them to fully love and appreciate us. All this we can do and hence experience happiness, without the possession of riches.

I don't need to tell you how many times wealthy persons have attested to the fact that money cannot buy real

Through the window of life, Fallacious Perception sees everything but the truth

happiness. They know it is true because where the benefits of riches are concerned, they have 'been there and done that' so to speak, and so proven to themselves the truthfulness of it. It would certainly be wise of us then to spare ourselves the misery of aspiring at all costs for riches based on the fallacious perception that it will bring our total happiness.

Insight On the Get-Rich-Quick Mentality (A by-product of this fallacious perception)

The get-rich-quick mentality stems from the concept that it is easier and sweeter if one can get something out of doing little or nothing at all. One possessing this mentality wishes to satisfy his material desires almost overnight without taking the traditional route of hard work. For this reason, the world is never short of gamblers, thieves, murderers, lottery companies, raffles, conmen and politicians.

It is little wonder though that this self-defeating way of thinking is so common in our society today. For example, look at what is taught to our subconscious minds by many of the movies, advertisements and television shows we devote so many hours to watching. In them we see men and women basking in the glory and the power of being filthy rich. They wear fine clothing and jewelry, eat at only the finest restaurants, and travel the world on their private jets or vacation on their private yachts. They are always being catered to or adored, respected or feared, admired or envied. Many times they appear to be happy or fulfilled, creating the illusion that where they are, is where everyone else ought to be if they too are to be happy.

What insidiously encourages the get-rich-quick mentality though, is the fact that in most cases, these movies and television shows fail to accentuate the hard work (unless by unrighteous means) that was put into the acquisition of these person's wealth. So the viewer (the one being subconsciously programmed) identifies only with the glory, not the pain and the sacrifices, the prize not the price. Their hearts and minds naturally desire what they see but no impression is made upon them as to the reality of how the wealth was obtained. Misled by this illusion, they are driven not to work honestly and hard nor to make sacrifices but instead to concoct whatever scheme they can to acquire that kind of wealth with as little effort and sacrifice as possible. This get-rich-quick mentality, no doubt, is a dangerous one. It easily leads to frustration, depression and demoralization when the victim will, even if it means hurting others and so damaging precious relationships, lower his level of humanity, his own moral standards, in order to do whatever it takes to become rich. This is one very detrimental course we would do well to avoid.

Fallacious Perception #3: *Not everyone in the world can have success. Some will. Some won't. "I have not really achieved anything* *of significance in my life, so therefore* ***I must be one of those who won't."***

This is probably the least obvious fallacy of the three that I will discuss. It doesn't sound much like a fallacy at all, but maybe instead like reasonable thinking. Well, it is true that not everyone in the world will have success. Yes, some will and some won't. But to assume that because you have not yet accomplished what you wish, that *you* are one of those persons, is no doubt a self-defeating fallacy. No one is predestined to fail. We are all a product of our own choices. As my father would always tell me when growing up, we choose our own destinies. None of us, including you, are ever totally hopeless in the way of accomplishing worthwhile goals in life. Perhaps it may take a little longer for you to achieve certain things than other persons you know, but the point is, we are all capable of achieving our goals, once they are realistic and reasonable. With careful planning, hard work, humility to recognize failure and to learn from it, endurance, determination and yes patience, you too can be added to the list of persons considered successful.

In Closing

There are several other examples of fallacious perceptions that we could discuss together. However, in order to sharpen your own ability to accurately perceive life's situations for yourself, personal private meditation and analysis is the platinum key. By quietly reasoning with yourself and asking questions to yourself of which you carefully discern the answers to, your conscious mind will gradually become aware of these fallacious perceptions and you can then rid them from it -- for good.

Just for fun though, let's log on to a 'website' of some more examples of fallacious perceptions at

'www.fallaciousperceptions.com'.

For the sake of being explicit, I have put in **bold print** the word or phrase in each sentence that reveals the fallacy in these commonly held perceptions.

'www.fallaciousperceptions.com'

- » Being human implies that one is **naturally inclined** to be humane.
- » An older head is **always** a wiser head.
- » Having good looks automatically makes one **special.**
- » All doctors are **bright.**
- » **Most persons** from the ghetto lack intellect.
- » A person who is constantly chirpy must be a **happy** individual.

- Sex is a **physiological** need.
- Once someone is set in his ways, it is **almost impossible** for him to change.
- You are **always, at all costs** obligated to your relatives.
- All who are generous to you **truly care** about your well being.
- Because you are good to others, others will **always** be good to you.
- Honest people are **weak.**
- It is **unhealthy** for one to still be unmarried at thirty.
- All children who throw tantrums are **spoiled.**
- There is **no meaning** to life.
- First impressions **always** last.
- **Most** persons in the mental health field are mentally healthy.
- **It is difficult** for persons having many friends or who are given much attention to suffer from a deep feeling of loneliness.

- Some people were **just born** evil, stupid, or 'out of luck'.
- There **is** such a thing as luck.
- Depth and maturity **must come** with adulthood.
- Marriage **must** bring happiness.
- One's past, **most likely**, will determine one's future.
- **All** elderly people are unexciting.
- Milk is **good** for you.
- **No one** enjoys pain.
- All university graduates are **well educated.**
- Most churchgoers are **God-fearing.**
- **All** babies are cute.☺

Chapter Six

Applied Imagination -- A Platinum Key!

The world is a tragedy to those who feel and a comedy to those who think.

William Shakespeare

Your mind, yes, the one *you* have is an extraordinarily wonderful and powerful instrument. If you could literally view what's inside it, in all its dimensions, there is no doubt that it would be an overwhelming and fascinating experience. You would see a seemingly infinite series of images, concepts, ideas and fantasies, all created based on your personal memories, experiences, perceptions and desires.

Now, your reading what I have just mentioned about your mind and what you might possibly see there, may have served to activate the very faculty of it that I wish to discuss. It is this faculty that enabled you to 'see' and so to conceptualize what I just said. It is your faculty of imagination.

Everyone having a brain, has the ability to imagine, to create mental pictures. Our imagination is expressed or made manifest in just about everything we do. The way we speak, the way we dress, the way we act. In fact our overall behavior and approach to life is greatly based, whether directly or indirectly, on this ability to imagine -- to mentally innovate -- to think.

Now, like all other skills or abilities, our ability to imagine must be nurtured and exercised regularly if it is to really be of great use to us. As one writer Gerard I. Nierenberg puts it: "Our rewards come not from having brains but in using them."

This means then that we will not be satisfied with merely being able to picture things mentally. Instead, we also want to advance and to be able to visualize just about *anything* in any proportion, dimension or form we choose; in a way that is unique to each of us. Still yet, we will want to take it a step further. We will want to be able to *manipulate* these mental images that we create, in order to make them really work for us.

Does this guy have an imagination or what?

This nurtured skill my friend, is the essence of psychological ingenuity and since it is done in the privacy of your own mind, there can be no mistakes, no pre-assigned restrictions and no embarrassments. Plus, the personal satisfaction you will experience will without a doubt be greatly rewarding.

Apart from enhancing your creative adeptness, there is a lot more that your trained imagination can do for you. Your imagination has the power to put you in immediate control of your thoughts and so of your emotions. As mentioned in Chapter Two, if we can manage to get our thoughts under control and thus become more mentally oriented, then consequently we will become more emotionally oriented as well; and as we will see, our imagination plays a key role in helping us to do so. Before looking at some fun examples of how we can apply our imagination to controlling ourselves psychologically and emotionally, let us first look at some necessary components of an effective imagination.

The Foundation of a Platinum Imagination

Fiction. If your imagination is to be effective, it cannot be based on logic or pure reality. Fiction -- unrealistic and illogical scenarios, representations, comparisons or illustrations -- are characteristic of an advanced imagination. This is so because unlike with common logic, it enables the desired ideas to be more easily exploited and manipulated and hence more profound and beneficial to the thinker.

Originality. There is nothing more boring than something lacking originality. And, if your imagination is boring it is as good as non-existent. You are the sole designer of your mind's thinking pattern, so, as you create your ideas and mental scenarios, perhaps even attaching personal symbolic meaning, be different, unique -- be original.

Explicity. Be explicit and bold in your imagination. Make your images graphic, dramatic, vivid and clear. Employ color, sound, smell, texture and taste if possible.

You will find that because of explicitness and the imperfect human mind, your imagination may sometimes become a little tasteless, morbid, even obscene. That is natural and in some specific cases it can work to your advantage. However, because of negative side effects it is important that the frequency of such imaginations be effectively regulated and kept under control.

Humor. Humor is unquestionably a platinum element of a healthy and effective imagination. Reason being, is that it serves two key purposes. One is that it enables the thinker to absorb and retain the desired idea quickly and easily. Hence, he will faster recall the idea if ever he needs to use it again. Secondly, it will simply make the thinker feel good, so attaching a positive emotion to the idea. This will be particularly useful in cases when the idea is used to control or counteract a negative thought or situation.

Activity. Think now of a cemetery or of a desert. Picture it for a few seconds. Stop. Now think of a circus! or a parade! See the point? Activity stimulates enthusiastic creativity, which is the essence of the imagination.

Simplicity. While your imagination should be creative, lively, and explicit, it is important that it doesn't become too complex, to the point where it feels overworked. You should never feel stressed because of exercising your imagination. Keep it easy, light and uncluttered. As the saying goes: Ingenuity enables simplicity and simplicity is genius.

Now, let's get to the fun stuff.

May the Best Feeling Win

Often times situations in life will test your self-control. Something will happen that might cause you to feel an influx of anger, fear or hurt that will tempt you to act accordingly.

As you know, the surge of every emotion comes because of the release of specific chemicals in the brain. So at those times when you feel yourself losing control, why not actually *picture* those specific chemicals, in your system fighting in their effort to take you over. Picture them as some evil, noisy little critters with a Tasmanian Devil-like personality trying to battle their way through your system. Visualizing this, or something to this effect, will immediately expose your mind to the reality of what actually happens when you are being emotionally challenged. Hence, you can simply counter it by imagining further, the positive little creatures representing your emotional control system, completely dominating (if even by violent means) the negative critters. Doing this may even add a little humor to the whole experience causing the negative feeling to subside.

Blocking the Entrances to Your Mind

In the same way that you bar your house with grills and locked doors to protect your body from harm, so too you must find a way to bar your psyche with 'grills' and 'locked doors' to protect your mind from harm.

There will be times when we find ourselves in situations that either directly or indirectly threaten our mind's health. It may be that we have to face someone who is verbally abusive, someone who deliberately tries to hurt or annoy us, control us, intimidate us, or to take away our self-confidence. It may also be that we are involuntarily exposed to something offensive or shocking, disturbing quarrels, eroticism, or violence. We can never have complete control over the things we see and hear but where the protection of our minds is concerned, we must at least have a plan.

Here again comes the use of the imagination. Picture your mind as having five steel doors that bar the entrances to it. Each of them may be connected to each of your senses. Now you are the only one that has control over when and for how long you will open any or all of these doors. No other human has the power to do this. There is only one master key that you possess at all times.

Now whenever those situations come up and you need to protect your mind from negative influences, imagine those steel doors of your mind slamming shut and preventing anything at all from entering. Not only must you visualize these doors being shut, but being barred and locked as well. Make it so vivid that you can even hear and feel the doors slam shut.

To aid you in making this tactic most effective, you can, when you are 'locking down', avoid paying attention to the source of the negative influence. Look away or close your eyes. Hear but do not listen. Fold your arms across your chest and if you're sitting, cross your legs. Doing these things will aid in shielding off the darts of negativity from your precious mind.

Like Water Off A Duck's Back

Have you ever heard someone, with the intention of expressing the triviality or simplicity of a task use the expression 'like water off a duck's back'? Well, you can do the same -- only you will picture it. Imagine any personal insult, minor setback, occasional distraction or any thing of that sort completely missing your head (and so your mind) and simply running off your back (behind you in the past) into the pond of life where you are floating comfortably.

Flushing It All Out

This fourth example of applied imagination may seem a little tasteless at first, but its application can prove to be very beneficial and I am almost certain you will never forget it.

"Hasta la vista – baby"

Every time you visit your toilet, you leave something undesirable behind. Isn't that true? Yes, with one flush you release what was once a detestable part of you, into virtual non- existence. You never see it again and it is never called to mind (until of course the next day or perhaps week, but that's another issue). Now, if we use our imagination we can apply this normal human function to dealing with undesirable minor problems and unnecessary burdens or sources of anxiety. How so? Try and visualize the *actual problems* being forcefully flushed down that same toilet into virtual non-existence where it can never return to you. Just as how you would not dwell on what you physically released, you will no longer be inclined to dwell on this problem that you will have psychologically and emotionally released. So you see, a wild imagination can indeed serve as a gentle laxative for psychological or emotional constipation. Happy flushing!

'It Could Be Worse'

Have you ever fallen victim to a bad experience and then have somebody tell you: "Never mind, it could have been worse"? Perhaps. Well how did it make you feel? Any better? Probably not. This is because in order for this statement to provide any real comfort for you, it must first be explicitly conceived in your psyche. It must be clearly perceived and accepted as a fact to you that *it really could have been worse* and nothing else can better help you do this than your own imagination.

I'll give you a personal example. About a year ago, I accidentally ran over my favorite puppy Ruff in my driveway. I was devastated. For days, I was immune to any words of comfort and I didn't know what to do. I went to see a friend of mine and I told him what happened. His comment was: "It could have been worse. It could have been a human being instead." At first, I thought he was being insensitive but at once my imagination tripped in. I begun visualizing my neighbor's two year-old son Matthew playing in my driveway; me reversing without seeing him and then crushing his little scull to pieces. I visualized blood and tissue everywhere and with it I heard screams of panic and fear. I visualized ambulances and the police and persons in the entire neighborhood running out in horror and distress. After visualizing this shocking scenario, though I was still sad at the loss of my dear puppy, I became instantly grateful to be in the position that I was in reality. By my imagination, I was able to thoroughly conceive the idea that *it really could have been worse* and being shaken up by the vivid images I produced in my mind, I was then ready to ease my grief, count my blessings and move on.

Here comes into effect the principle of relativity. Things only seem bad *when compared to how they were before* a negative occurrence. If you use your imagination to create a worst case scenario, then when compared to your present situation, things won't seem so bad after all. For every negative situation, you will see that it really can be much worse. Try it -- it will work for you.

Not Sure If You Can Do It?

Are there times when you could really use an extra boost of motivation or encouragement? Certainly. Perhaps then, you are a little intimidated by a challenge or you doubt your personal capability to successfully meet it. Wouldn't it be wonderful if at those times you could receive some kind of scientific measurement of your true capability, that could be used to let you know for sure if you are up to the challenge or not? Well here's some good news. You can! Remember, anything is possible, in your imagination.

Simply picture three or four scientists in a little isolated booth. Also in this booth, are futuristic equipment including a supercomputer with someone at the keyboard, as well as a supertelescope that is by some means always focused on you and on your life. Now, these scientists have been observing you since your birth, and they, somehow have full scientific knowledge of all that you are capable of.

Application? Well, whenever you are in doubt of your personal capability to succeed at something, simply imagine these scientists observing you through their telescope as you are having your doubts. While watching you, though, they are smiling with each other, slowly shaking their heads and saying in low tones: "If their was only some way we could tell him (or her) that he is more than capable of doing it. He has more than enough capabilibytes, not to mention potentiabytes" ☺ And, with that, they are all hoping that you will muster up the courage to face your challenge since they have scientific reason to be confident in you. All you have to do now -- is not waste that opportunity.

Stamp It Out

Have you ever had a bad thought or idea just pop in your mind when you least desire or expect it? Perhaps it keeps popping up during the day only causing you to be distracted. Well, whenever the negative thought surfaces, try imagining a huge, heavy stamp of a red "X" being loudly stamped over the thought. That "X" will symbolize prompt, complete rejection of the negative thought.

Shrinking a Monster

Has an emotionally stressful person ever bombarded you? Say, an angry boss, a miserable spouse, or a persistent complainer? Why not on those occasions use your imagination to picture this person as some kind of giant monster perhaps with many ugly heads and long salivating tentacles trying to eat you alive. You may just find yourself being amused at your private image instead of reacting negatively to this person's behavior. You can even take it a step further by imagining that this person is rapidly shrinking into a far away dungeon of unimportance. Try it. It can really serve as a protection from destructive emotional confrontations. Your reaction may even abate the behavior of your attacker. But most of all -- it's extremely fun!

"Goodness, she's even uglier than I thought!"

"Will You Be Joining Us Today?"

Do you remember the last time you were on the verge of a self-defeating reaction or behavior? Perhaps it was to get angry, to feel insulted and retaliate, to wallow in depression (as a pig wallows in mud), or to give in to fear. Well, the next time that happens, try this:

Imagine that there is this hallway, with doors on either side. You walk through this hallway every day of your life. Now, one of its doors opens to a room having only psychologically and emotionally dysfunctional people. They are all a part of an exclusive club in which they admit only victims like themselves. However, they observe outsiders (you and me) constantly, and whenever they see any of us displaying dysfunctional behavior, they attempt to invite us in that room to join their club.

So now, whenever you feel like you are about to behave in some way dysfunctional, simply imagine that as you are passing that door, it opens, then a Victim Club member sticks his head out and asks desperately: "Will you be joining us today?" How you choose to behave at that moment will serve as your answer to him. You will either decide to ignore him -- or you will decide to go in and sign up.

Note please, that in the case of this particular method, you may not need to picture the entire scenario every time you need self-control. Once ever may be good enough, since the aim is for you to establish, at those times, the idea that their does exist a dysfunctional class of people. They are identified by self-defeating characteristics, and this class is one you want to be no part of.

Like A Dog Returning To Its Vomit

Bad habits, often times are difficult to break. And so, when we do manage to break one of them, we feel a sense of personal accomplishment and we want never to repeat the habit again.

But what can we do whenever we are tempted to do so? Well, think of a dog returning to its vomit. By doing so, it is taking back in the waste it previously managed to eject from its system. Disgusting not to mention unhealthy isn't it? Need I say more?

Applying the Principle of Relativity

Think of something you knew as a small child. Perhaps some toy, an article of clothing, or even someone you still know. Back then their sizes seemed great in comparison to yours, right? But now they all seem much smaller. Why? -- Simply because *you've gotten bigger*! Yes, it is true. The bigger you get, the smaller things seem.

Now this principle of relativity can easily be used to 'rise' above a difficult situation making it seem much smaller than it is deemed initially. Whenever a challenging situation comes up, simply imagine yourself instantly advancing in experience, maturity, and emotional and psychological toughness, so much so that this problem can no longer be tough enough or challenging enough to seriously affect you.

In effect it becomes trivial when matched up to your 'newly formed' capability.

"Curtains please!"

At those times when absolute mental focus is needed, imagine your mind as being a theatre. Then, watch the curtains all around it being slowly drawn down, allowing absolutely nothing foreign to what's going on on stage (what you are focusing on) to enter.

"This Too Shall Pass"

One of the mistakes we often make whenever we are feeling, uncomfortable, confused, disturbed or depressed, is to give in to the idea that our present feeling will never go away. But instead of victimizing himself with this fallacious perception, there is something that one exercising his imagination can do. He can, at those times, visualize the bigger picture of his existence. That is, while he must do what is reasonably in his power to remedy the situation, he can, at the same time, imagine himself a few hours from then feeling happy and positive. (Hours and not minutes or seconds because it is more realistic and so easier to accept, that a limited but sufficient time is made available in order to work over any negative experience). He can even visualize himself telling someone else of his 'past' feeling or experience as if it

He's really out-of-it now, but he can see that it is just a matter of time before he will be fine again

is already just a recollection. In other words, a person can use his imagination to 'live' his desired future, in effect, 'speeding up' the process of surpassing his present moments which at times may be distressing or unpleasant. He can use his imagination to make his present moment seem like a past one.

What's Dead Is Dead

Is it challenging at times to avoid dwelling on negative or self-defeating memories? Yes. At those times, an immediate and effective remedy is needed. How about this? You know that if you bury a dead animal, after a while it will decay and start to stink, right? That being the case, would you ever want to dig up the corpse just to take a whiff of its odor? I certainly hope not. And, bringing up and dwelling on a past negative memory, (a dead experience) can be likened to doing just that. (By the way, if your answer to my last question was 'yes' I recommend that you stop reading this book right now and go and get yourself some more advanced help) Just as you would want to forget that dead animal and not even experience the results of its decay, so too you should want to disregard and forget the self-defeating memory.

So, whenever your self-defeating memory pops up, immediately mentally associate it with digging up and sniffing a rotting animal and just as you will find that repulsive, so too you will be turned off by dwelling on the negative memory.

Knowing Your Ups And Downs

Our level of personal capability at any point in time, is determined by a combination of factors. Factors such as mental and physical energy, emotional balance and perhaps the level of our spirituality. The levels of these factors vacillate constantly, in effect, regularly changing our level of personal efficiency. They can be affected by health, time of day, hunger, the weather or temperature, the day's events, lack of rest, or in a woman's case PMS.

Now, being able to picture these factor levels shifting, can certainly be helpful whenever you need personal power. How so? It will help you to have an immediate awareness and respect for what your present capabilities are and also reveal to you the factors you might need to improve or focus on at those particular times.

One way in which you can picture this is by thinking of an 'x' by 'y' chart depicting the levels, from minimum to maximum, of the individual factors. The towers representing the levels of the various factors shift up and down according to changes in your personal efficiency. With this chart, the thinker is able to recognize and compare the levels of the different factors that may at that time be determining his personal efficiency. He can then more readily exercise reasonableness in his approach to whatever he has to do at that particular moment.

The Mind Bubble

Whenever you have difficulty relaxing or falling asleep because of mental insomnia -- constantly thinking about the day's events or tomorrow's activities -- think of your mind as being a softly glowing bubble. It is pure and still and it refuses to be contaminated or disrupted by any of the invasive thoughts.

Would You Like To Restart? Click: 'Yes'

Have you ever had the experience when your mind suddenly becomes flooded with all kinds of thoughts that cause you to feel confused and disoriented? Well at those moments, try to instantly think of your mind as being a scrambled television screen. Think only of that screen and the "sssshhh..." sound that it makes. Then -- imagine the screen suddenly going blank -- then a few seconds later, one by one, organized ideas appear. That imagery will represent a clearing of your mind (a 'restarting', or 'rebooting') and then you can proceed to deal with the necessary thoughts more effectively, in an organized way.

Have The Last Laugh

Roger C. Anderson once made a wonderful and realistic statement that can be very reassuring when it is really thought about. He said: "Accept that some days you're the pigeon, and some days you're the statue."

On your down days, instead of dwelling on the negative aspects and harboring regret or resentment, picture Roger's comment and *you*, rather than the day, may just end up having the last laugh. See, I helped you out a little by using this depiction.

He's enjoying the last laugh

Final Thoughts

From these simple examples, it can be seen that the effective use of the imagination can certainly work to our advantage. Try and think of some ways in which you can enhance and expand yours. Try to think how you can manipulate ideas and images to make them work for you psychologically and emotionally. There are so many unique and creative ways, if only you should spend the time to think about them.

You will find that by your advancing and applying your imagination, your memory, as well as your sense of humor will improve significantly. However, here is a word of caution: there is a thin line between intelligently exercising a healthy imagination and idly practicing obsessive daydreaming. You must remain ever aware of the difference and completely avoid the latter as it is unhealthy and a waste of precious time.

In closing, I will leave you with a thought expressed by a man whose creative imagination earned him an indelible mark in human history. It is a thought that you yourself may come to have as you advance in creative thinking. He said: *A thought that sometimes makes me hazy; am I or are the others crazy*? Perhaps you've heard about him. His name was Albert Einstein.

Chapter Seven

Platinum Keys To Further Advancement

*Whatever you are, be a **great** one.*

Anonymous

Like the building blocks used to construct a powerful, impressive tower, there exists fundamental 'blocks' in the form of practices and qualities. These are needed in order to construct a fortified, efficient and enduring emotional, mental or psychological system. These practices and qualities when learned and implemented, will help in minimizing the self-defeating problems that commonly affect us.

Now, the 'cement' used to form these blocks is primarily based on accurate perception, discernment and experience; all of which we learn and gain from life and the choices we decide to make on our own. Consequently, it is more or less through life that we learn to improve ourselves, by making constant adjustments and modifications to our personal way of thinking and so to our personal qualities and practices.

Neither space, nor time, nor my own personal capability will allow me to discuss all of the necessary building blocks. But, in addition to the ones discussed so far in this book, I will now draw attention to a few more fundamental ones. I would like to suggest though that as you read them, pause after each section for a minute or two to think about how you can personally apply the recommendation. You can even make your own improvements or additions to them if you desire. Shall we continue?

What Do You Expect?

Whatever you expect to happen is determined by the thoughts you dwell upon plus the intensity of the emotions behind those thoughts.

Dr. Robert Anthony

Positive expectations are essential in one's effort to build confidence and so to experience success. If you are the sort to always expect the worst, or even less than the best, then you can kiss the hope of success good-bye from now, because it is virtually impossible for you.

In order to expect success you should not only think positively but *feel* positively as well. You will need to control your thoughts and emotions by taking full charge of what you tell yourself, whether verbally, by means of your mental pictures, or by your actions and reactions. Taking charge in this way is necessary and should be done consistently, before you can become inclined to having positive expectations.

Also, simply telling yourself what you expect from you is meaningless *if you really don't expect it* and so it is mandatory that positive thoughts become a genuine part of your psyche.

To illustrate: I can recall a boxing match that took place several years ago. It was between Mike Tyson and a huge man named Bruce Seldon. I remember seeing Seldon on TV boasting about what he expected to do in the fight and that Tyson didn't stand a chance against him. He kept telling the world and no doubt himself this for months, but all was in vain. For did he *really* believe what he was saying? Did he *really* have positive expectations for his match? He couldn't have! If he did, chances are he would have at least lasted one round in the fight -- which he did not. The result only confirmed to him what he already knew: he was fearful of his opponent (fear being the 'intense emotion behind the thought' of fighting Tyson) and so he did not expect much of himself or of his ability to win.

This tells us something else: when we *genuinely* have positive expectations, modesty should become a by-product. You need not try to convince anyone of your confidence or positivity. It should be a personal, private, self-satisfying experience reflected only in a quiet dignity. The results will speak for themselves. So with your best efforts in life, expect only the best and the best, in one way or another, at some point in time, will come to you. Speaking of time...

Make Time Your Close Personal Friend

One of the main attributes of a good friend is that he or she can be counted on no matter what, am I right? Sure. What about time? Well, as you know, time has no beginning neither can it have an end so it will always be here. It is sure to pass. Look at your clock. Let's say it says 12:25. You know that it's only a matter of 60 seconds for it to become 12:26. Sixty seconds later, 12:27 and so on. Even if you should remove the clock's battery, 60 seconds later time will still increase by a minute and will continue to do so forever and ever and ever.

So what does this mean for us? Well, just as we do with other natural and predictable occurrences we should develop a respect and an appreciation for the passage of time. It cannot be speeded up and it cannot be slowed down; it's simply there and the deeper we can fathom the experience and significance of it is the better off we will be.

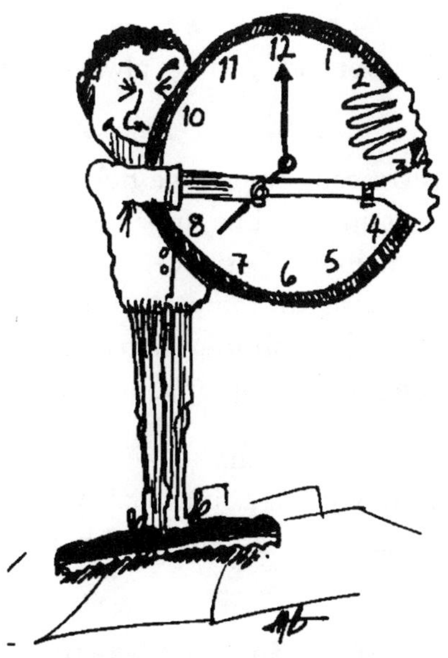

"Time – you mean so much to me."

To help us to do so, we can use our imagination to think of time as an infinitely long rope. Now think of a point on the rope and label it using the year you were born. Now, from that point on there are formed several other points that represent your days of life along with your experiences, accomplishments, changes, growth and so on, up until now. Now, these points are fixed (you cannot change what has already taken place in your life) and because you are still alive means that there are several other points (accomplishments, changes, experiences and so on), yet to come. Now remember, time never ends and so these points, for as long as you're alive, will never end. You can always count on them to occur.

Now using this concept, we can be helped to appreciate the value of the passing of time and hence cultivate that seemingly elusive quality of **patience**. Whether long term patience (for instance, waiting for weeks, months or years for something to take place). Or short-term patience (e.g. waiting in line for something or waiting for someone to arrive).

Fully appreciating the fact that *things will happen in time* (you *must* move from point to point to point) can help us to exercise greater patience in our lives with regards to our expectations.

Simply visualize the time rope. See where you are presently on it in relation to the 'point' you want to be at. Then when you see it you will realize that anxiety is needless since it is *just a matter of time* before you arrive there. Even if you have no idea where the point is, or how far away you are from it, at least you know that it *must be there somewhere* along the rope. And so, waiting only means that you have more time to *prepare* for it or to do other things.

Whenever you find yourself in a situation where you need to exercise patience, along with using the imaginary rope, you can calmly and reassuringly remind yourself that it's *only a matter of time* before you accomplish what you wish.

I will leave you with a few examples of some things that you might say at those times, but before I do, I really want to encourage you to practice this method of cultivating patience. The more you do, believe me, the easier it will become for you to exercise patience. Now, back to those things you might tell yourself.

» In time, this problem will be corrected.

» In time, I will see the solution to my problem.

» In time, this pain must lessen and eventually end.

» In time, I will reach the front of the line.

» In time, I will have more experience.

» In time, I will be better.

» In time, I will have what I need.

» In time, this person I am waiting on will arrive and explain his lateness to me.

» In time, I will understand all this.

» In time, I will be over this and it will no longer mean a thing to me.

» In time, my being stuck here in traffic will be a thing of the past and I will be in the comfort of my home.

- In time, in one way or another, I will be rewarded for my hard efforts.
- In time, I will forget this ever happened.
- In time, I will be wiser.
- In time, justice will prevail.

Humility Means Power

Humility, according to the Webster's New Dictionary, is defined as 'the state of being lowly; unpretentious; modest; to bring oneself down in condition or rank.' Unfortunately in this world, it is a quality grossly lacking since it is in many cases associated with the poor, the sick, the so-called unimportant or with persons weak in character. Well, it is true that most of such persons appear humble. Perhaps they have very little choice but to. But what about accomplished, privileged or powerful people? Can they too really be humble?

Why, certainly. In fact quite a few have managed to accomplish this. How? They have come to understand the true meaning of what it is to be humble. These unique persons are able to be humble, firstly because they have gained insight and wisdom. They have learned to respect the value of life and humanity. They are persons confident in themselves and in their personal capabilities and unlike the rest of the world, they do not use their accomplishments to define themselves. They have nothing to prove to the world and they have so much self-love and self-respect that it in no way hurts them to put others first, or to honor and respect lowly-ranked persons. Persons such as these are so powerful that they have successfully brought themselves above and beyond the every-day impressive things of this world; whether riches, higher education, good looks, fame and so on. Persons having such things cannot arouse in these advanced people any envy or intimidation and if they themselves possess wealth, higher education or fame, they feel absolutely no desire to be proud since they are not fascinated by any of these things. A truly humble person sees these things for just what they are and silently laughs at the ones haughty over them. What is *he* fascinated with? Building morale, character, virtue, inner strength and solid loving relationships with other human beings. *These things* he holds in high esteem. And, incidentally these things he finds easy to do since genuine humility has as side effects, patience, endurance, and a calm, easy-going spirit.

So you see, there is a lot more to humility than the commonly held perception of it. It is something worth cultivating as it brings true value to life. Yes, humility brings wisdom and insight, it brings peace of mind and self-confidence; it means less stress to our souls, it means simplicity and control and yes, humility means power.

Organization and Moderation

For any unit to run successfully and efficiently, it must first be properly organized. Therefore, if you intend to enhance your general performance in life it would do you well to organize yourself as best as you can and to maintain that organization.

When one is organized, not only does it make functioning a pleasure, but also it lessens the chances of blunders and oversights which are common whenever there is disorganization. So, start by organizing your area of personal space. Your bedroom, living room, kitchen. What about your work area? Your desk, your files, your tools? Do you have a daily planner or organizer? Are there bits and pieces of paper sticking or falling out of it? Then what's the point? Organize it neatly and write in it legibly. In summary -- organize your life.

Now, there is another important quality that deserves mention. That of moderation; avoiding extremes and keeping plans and activities within reasonable limits. Do not go overboard in anything that you do -- even if it is a good thing. Maintain balance and learn to cut yourself some slack every now and again. Moderation is platinum if you are to maintain happiness while dealing with your responsibilities, so indeed it must be borne in mind when planning your life's affairs.

Be Like the Little Train That Could

A very common dilemma even among bright, talented persons, is the lack of diligence, persistence, determination, a fighting spirit, and an ability to finish what is started. Persons with this problem are often dissatisfied with their lives as they remain in or even below the plain of mediocrity. They sometimes can't see why they can never accomplish the things they wish, because as far as they're concerned all their efforts seem to be in vain.

There are various reasons for these persons being the way they are. Let's look at a few and we can see if any of them apply to us.

» They may take for granted their natural abilities, gifts or talents.

» They may be afraid of failure.

» They may be too easily distracted.

» They may lack balance and moderation and so take on too many functions and aspirations at once.

» They may lack self-will, giving up at the first sign of difficulty.

» They may lack focus, forgetting if even for brief moments, what their goals are.

» They may lack motivation. They may see no reason for doing what they're doing and so put in only half-hearted efforts.

» They may lack patience, becoming quickly discouraged by not seeing the immediate results of their efforts.

» They may be just plain lazy.

The Little Train That Could – did.

If you are a person lacking diligence, it doesn't matter what the reason is; there are things you can do to overcome this obstacle. I struggled with this for most of my life but I have learned many ways to overcome it. Here are a few.

» Ask for support. Let persons close to you in on your problem and let them help you.

» Create motivation. Use your imagination and come up with ways in which you can motivate yourself.

» Make up visual reminders of your goals, (notes, posters, bookmarkers etc)

» ***Very important:*** Write down all your goals and then use modesty and discernment to determine which are of greatest importance. Recognize that *you can't do them all* and so swallow your superfluous ambition, maybe even your pride and delete, or at least postpone, the less important ones. Choose a select few and direct your focus toward only those.

» Make strict time allotments for activities related to your goal.

» Think of a game that you are not very experienced in. Perhaps Tennis, Chess or Scrabble. Deliberately play it with someone who is good at it and who will very likely beat you. This can be a tough challenge but it will serve as an excellent exercise in endurance and patience. Before you begin the game, promise yourself that come what may, you are going to fight right to the end. You will not give up. This exercise will help to cultivate in you a more mature and advanced attitude toward your more important goals.

» Stick with people who are diligent, consistent, determined, and who usually finish whatever they start.

Advancement Through Self-Intimacy

To be self-intimate means that one has a close relationship with him or herself. A self-intimate person is constantly in touch with his thoughts and feelings and is always cognizant of his desires, aims and motivations.

A person, by means of self-intimacy, tries as best as he can to keenly and sensitively understand himself. He does so not simply for the sake of knowledge, but with the aim of knowing how best to take care of himself, improve himself, accept himself and then protect himself.

Please do not confuse a self-intimate person with a self-obsessed or self-absorbed person. The latter is superficial, dysfunctional and proud; the former is more likely to be down-to-earth and humble.

Self-intimate people, because they are more emotionally and psychologically aware than others, tend to have a deeper, more advanced level of sensitivity to the needs of others. Hence, they always make better comforters, acceptors, listeners, empathizers, discerners, forgivers, and lovers.

So how can we become more self-intimate? Well, we can start by regularly spending quality time alone. We can use this time to think about our different experiences and the psychological and emotional effects they have on us. We can reflect upon the many positive lessons we have learned thus far and check to see if we are putting them to good use. This time can also be spent to think about our flaws and to see if we can possibly make efforts to get rid of them or at least to reduce them. We can also reflect on our loved ones and on ways we can improve our relationships with them. Also, we can reminisce about our positive childhood experiences or about important milestones in our lives. The point is, we use this time to think about our complete selves in relation to the quality of our lives.

Even though this time is important, it should not be too long. In fact, regularly spending prolonged periods of time by yourself can lead to self-insulation and selfishness. The times you spend alone in deep meditation should be no more than, say, three to five hours per week, more, only at those times when it is really necessary.

For your intimate moments, it is important that the atmosphere is conducive to thinking. Perhaps you may want to go outside or by a window near to plants, flowers or a natural body of water. Very soft instrumental music may help, as well as dead silence if that's better for you. Petting a calm pet is also very conducive to deep thinking. But whatever aids you choose for enhancing your intimate moments are totally up to you. Just as long as you are comfortable, relaxed and at peace with yourself.

What Can You Do Punchinello Little Fellow?

Having a wholesome hobby is an excellent way to build a feeling of self-worth and self- esteem. It is definitely a channel to self-improvement not to mention a great stress management technique.

So what can *you* do? What have you tried? Is there anything that interests you that you think you may want to learn? Any particular skill you want to develop? How about playing a musical instrument? Crocheting or knitting? Making floral arrangements or cooking? Art or Craft? Designing, gardening, writing? There are so many hobbies to choose from.

It would suit you better however, to choose at least one hobby that stimulates your creative ability such as the ones just suggested. Choose something that will excite your imagination. Also, do something that you can share with others, something that is an expression of the unique you.

Psychomusical Connections

Have you ever had the experience of hearing an old familiar song and having it bring back certain memories to your mind? Memories perhaps of your childhood days, your first romance or even of something tragic that happened in the past? All sorts of emotions may have without warning rushed into your system and caused you to think about the things you were reminded of. Depending on the profundity of the memories, the experience could well have set the tone of your mood for hours, days, maybe longer.

Yes, music has this power. The power to take our minds and hearts back in time. It has the power to incite us to relive past experiences; those we always want to remember and even those we want desperately to forget.

What is the secret to music's power? Well, music, being rhythmic sound, can easily permeate the subconscious mind and form an association or connection with any thought or feeling that one may experience. This way it can serve as a figurative camera or recorder of these experiences.

So how else apart from the obvious can this fact work to our advantage? Well, instead of involuntarily registering random psychomusical connections, why not voluntarily create specific positive connections for yourself? How? Well, you know the kind of music you like. Suppose you want to preserve say, a joyful, exciting experience: choose one of your favorite songs that you have recently discovered. ('Recently' because you don't want a song that you may have without realizing it, already connected feelings and thoughts to.) Now, while you are having that joyful experience, play and replay the song as often as you can and make sure that your entire environment is as conducive to your joyful thoughts and feelings as possible. Now, to effectively preserve this experience, repeat this as often as you can using this same song. Do *not* play this song at any other time other than when you are having joyful, exciting thoughts and feelings.

After you have mastered this exercise and your subconscious mind has firmly established this song as your 'happy song'; you can then use it occasionally to cheer you up whenever you get depressed.

Apart from creating 'happy songs', this method can be used to create other different kinds as well. There can be 'comforter songs', 'confidence builder songs', deep thinker songs', dominant focus songs', 'romantic songs', or 'hard worker songs'. Whatever mode you want to set your mind in you can create a corresponding song for it.

Remember, these songs that you 'create' for yourself will be your own private stimulants, so keep them very personal to you.

So you see, you can use the power of music to work greatly to your advantage. Try this fun technique -- it may just work for you.

Pump Up Those Mental Muscles

Mental fitness plays a significant role in personal advancement. And, as with the physical body, regular exercise is the key to achieving mental fitness.

Being out of school or having a simple, routine or mechanical job is no excuse for being mentally lazy or out of shape. We should always try to keep our minds in shape by testing and improving our thinking skills.

Some ways in which we can do this are as follows:

1. Practice doing mathematical calculations in your head rather than always reaching for the calculator.
2. Challenge brain teasers or riddles and don't give up too easily.
3. Engage in fun, interesting word games by forming other words from words, doing crossword puzzles, playing Boggle, Scrabble, or any other game that encourages you to think with words.
4. Exercise and improve your memory skills. Try to memorize telephone numbers, people's names, your grocery list, places et cetera instead of always depending on pen and paper.
5. Even if you don't actually do an IQ test, why not get one of those IQ self-test books and have some

fun with the questions? You may just surprise yourself.

6 Play or learn to play strategic board games such as Chess, Checkers, or Backgammon.

Avoid Watching Too Much TV

TV obliterates the very distinction, the very line, between reality and unreality.

The Unreality Industry

Do you happen to know a TV addict? Stop and think about that person for a minute. Is he or she bright, imaginative, innovative? Is he or she hardworking, mentally independent, serious-minded? Is he or she realistic in terms of thinking? Nine out of ten I'm sure, the answer is 'no' for most if not all of these questions.

The reason for this is simple. Excessive TV watching, because it discourages mental innovation and creativity, promotes a mental laziness even a dullness that can easily program the victim into a mode of non-progressiveness. In essence, the TV becomes like the brain of the addict. It does the thinking for him and produces in him the kind of excitement and fascination that if he only gave it a chance, his own mind independently could.

So, while there are wonderfully educational, informative and entertaining programs to be seen on television, it would be wise for us to approach our TV viewing habits with strict discernment and moderation. A truly advanced person does not need the television to fill any void in his life; he needs only his mind to do so.

Say No To Gossip

Average minds discuss events,
Brilliant minds discuss ideas,
***Small** minds discuss **people**.*

Wise Old Saying

Quit Addictions

Whether it is to food, alcohol, sex, nicotine, hard drugs, television, fantasizing, partying or even working, addiction is a dangerous illness. Not just because it is self-destructive, but because it can take a powerful hold on both mind and body.

Addiction is in most cases difficult to break. This is because the addict's abuse of whatever he is addicted to produces in his insecure mind a false sense of security and control while fostering an illusion of escape for those few moments of satisfaction. Consequently, he always feels that he *needs* this thing and so he always seeks to have it. Now there are several programs for addicts of different sorts including the well known 12-step program. But I'll now tell you my own *3-step* program that is very effective for anyone who *truly and seriously wants to* quit his addiction.

Step #1

In one of your 'sober' moments, recognize that your addiction has made you into an enslaved, out of control animal. It has held you captive to its power. A power that doesn't even exist. You can never truly be in possession of your own mind until you break this addiction because it will continue to rule you for as long as you let it. Now, you may not yet see it, but **there does exist inside of you tremendous capability to abandon your addiction. Once you're human, you do have this capability**. Now re-read these words in bold print twice and I want you to nod your head slowly while you read them. Okay, fine.

Step #2

Imagine yourself sitting in a cold, wet, smelly, grungy and uncomfortable room where there is very little light. There are sounds of pain and despair, but you cannot quite see the source. Pause for a second now and really get a vivid picture of this in your mind. Alright. Now, in this room, you are sitting around a table across from a giant of a man having several steel chains, locks and keys. But, on the table in front of you there is a contract. This contract states:

This is to verify that I **(state your name)** *have decided to exercise my single right to abandon this prison permanently and to enter a place of freedom . I am tired of the guilt, of the pain I am experiencing, and I have no more time or energy to waste. My mind can no longer accept this sub-human existence and so I must leave and can never return.*

"So, ya bustin' out a this place huh? I always knew you didn't quite fit in aound here."

Now see yourself signing the contract along with two healthy, happy, witnesses who represent an organization of a free people and who are excitedly cheering you on. If you wish, you can even draft up a real one and sign it in front of real witnesses.

Step #3

Acknowledge that even though you may strongly desire to quit your addiction, there will still be painful *but temporary* withdrawal symptoms experienced. So expect them. What you need to now do is fill the newly formed gap in your mind with constructive, upbuilding activity. All that displaced drive and energy must now be directed toward something else. Recognize too that should you relapse occasionally into your former habit, you will *still* be making progress. It doesn't mean that you're back in that 'place'. Just *honestly* and carefully consider the situation that may have led you to relapse each time and make any necessary adjustments with the view to avoiding the cause as best as you can. Also, tell trusted non-addict friends about your efforts and ask them for their help. With that, avoid the company of those having your former addiction.

Congratulations! You have just learned a Sure Enough 3-step program to overcoming addiction. If you need to, why don't you try it? It may just work for you.

Take Zero Things for Granted

Admittedly, all of us are guilty of the terrible crime of taking things for granted. But, in a court of reason, we could easily plead ignorance since in truth and in fact, we are most times unaware of committing this crime.

The fact is, there are a great many things in life for us to savor and appreciate; but because of the even greater number of annoyances and difficulties we come across, we easily become distracted from these things and tend to give more attention to dealing with the negatives.

We must know however, that a big part of being advanced as a person is being able to consciously appreciate as many of the positives in life as we can.

Take a look at this list of things that we commonly take for granted. Then, see if there is anything that you think you may personally be taking for granted. After which, decide to make a conscious effort to show more appreciation for these things. Openly recognize and acknowledge the value of them, thereby learning to take zero things for granted.

» Indoor running water

» The use of your limbs

» Your sight, hearing or ability to speak

» The smile of a stranger

- Sunlight and rain
- Your parents
- The kind of influence you have on others
- Compliments
- Your health and sanity
- Your daily meals
- The attention or company of others
- Time
- Your life lessons
- Your friendships
- The gift of life (all you bungie jumpers and daredevils☺)
- Your home
- Your teeth
- Nature
- Living creatures

No Man is an Island

It does not matter how mentally, psychologically or emotionally advanced you are. If you are not exposed to other loving, caring, solid and upbuilding human beings, do not kid yourself -- it will not last very long. The truth of the matter is, you do need others. As the saying goes: *No man is an island so no man can stand alone.*

In light of this fact, we must constantly strive, in a spirit of humility, to maintain loving relationships with others around us. How? Well Mr. Benjamin Franklin said how when he said: *If you would be loved,* love and be lovable. The next chapter will discuss how to do just this.

Chapter Eight

Platinum Keys To Loving Your Loved Ones

You will find as you look upon your life, that the moments that you have really lived are the moments when you have done things in the spirit of love.

Henry Drummond

During one of our many intimate discussions, a disheartened girlfriend of mine confessed to me that she has a very strong desire to express love but is intimidated by the possible loss incurred from loving others. "Why do you think that is?" I asked her. After a long pause, she said, "I don't think I have what it takes, it's too much of a personal sacrifice." Her feeling of inadequacy shows that there is at least one important thing that she was able to discern about love and that is that it really does involve great personal sacrifice to the one loving. It goes beyond just a strong liking or a passionate affection for another person. Love encompasses a complete genuine appreciation and respect for another person's whole existence.

Loving someone would then call for the devoting of much time and energy to caring for that one both psychologically and emotionally, with the view to helping him (or her) attain and maintain joy and satisfaction in his life. This in turn means being able to discern and respond to the specific needs and peculiarities of the loved one. Doing so by taking into consideration his likes and dislikes, his interests and goals, his level of accomplishment, his level of maturity, sensitivity and his general lifestyle. All this, in order to have a genuine picture of his true self, rather than his superficial role in the relationship.

In order to achieve this deep understanding of the loved one, enough time and energy need to be invested in the relationship. And, of course, the extent to which this is done depends greatly on the nature of the relationship. That is to say that if your loved ones consist of say your parents, children, siblings, mate, friends and neighbors, the amount of time you spend and the level of obligation you feel toward each will naturally differ. You may feel a deeper sense of personal obligation toward your children than say toward your siblings; your marriage mate than toward your friends and so on. Apart from that fact, each person is completely different from the next and hence unique approaches will be needed to effectively care for each one.

In no way do I intend to imply that loving someone effectively is a difficult task that requires special intelligence. Not at all. In fact, all that are needed is simply the *willingness* to love and the *awareness* that there is more involved in loving someone than just a strong liking or caring for that person. This willingness and awareness are enough for you to automatically become more empathetic, discerning, and sensitive to the needs of others. They will engage your subconscious mind to seek out and to learn each one's individual needs and to respond accordingly. However, as we move on in this chapter we will briefly discuss five platinum keys that may make it even easier for you to develop this level of awareness and empathy and so be on your way to mastering the delicate art of loving your loved ones.

Respect Each Person's Uniqueness

It is important that we acknowledge the uniqueness that exists among us human beings. In the same way that we all possess completely different fingerprints, we each possess a completely different avenue of existence. One that is uniquely our own. This is to say that we each go about experiencing life through different eyes. Seeing things differently. Feeling things differently. No one else in the world can experience life in *exactly* the same way as you do.

It is impossible because you are, like I am, a complete prototype of a human being. Failure to recognize and accept this fact may only give rise to intolerance, selfishness and unreasonable expectations of other people, including and especially our loved ones. Of course, this may easily result in the crippling of our relationships with them.

It means less stress for us, if instead of trying to change our loved ones or force them to adjust on our road of existence, we accept and respect the fact that they have their own unique roads. They have already made and will continue to make choices for themselves that allow them to define their own personality traits, values, goals, standards, tastes and so on.

One way to develop an appreciation for the uniqueness of each human is to make conscious efforts to closely observe others in groups. Perhaps when you're walking on a crowded street, socializing or working in a group, spending time with your family or any similar activity. If we observe closely, the way they each look, their sizes, their shapes, their distinctive voices, the way they express themselves, the way they laugh, walk and dress, we can almost feel the uniqueness of each individual as they naturally travel on their own avenues of existence. That being so, we can look forward to interacting with others, in particular our loved ones, deeming each relationship as unique and special; deeming it a privilege to come in contact with another inimitable human being. This should then incite us to seek out different ways of building our relationships with our loved ones.

Something as basic as cultivating the ability to appreciate different kinds of say, music, foods and cultures will also make us more conducive to appreciating the differences in and the uniqueness of each person.

Expect the Expected

What does this mean? Say for instance you are baby-sitting your friend's two year-old child. The child sees his bottle which happens to be standing beside your favorite vase. He, without your help, reaches for the bottle and hits the vase over smashing it to pieces. How do you respond? Are you angry? If so, angry at whom or what? If you really stop and think about it, it would be ridiculous of you to be angry at little Tommy. After all, he's two years old! Sure you're hurt that your vase was destroyed, but Tommy's level of awareness and self-control is much less than yours, so -- what else could you have reasonably expected? The point of this is that the same principle applies to everyone of any age. Expectations of each person (because they are uniquely different), should be different. Never should we commit the folly of using our own standards to judge others and so assume that everyone is capable of doing the things we desire of them in exactly the way we desire them to be done. If Mr. Jones is a known drunkard, why should you feel offended or angry when he runs out into the street in only his underwear screaming obscenities? If your child is in Grade 4, but his level of understanding is really still at Grade 2, why should you be surprised or upset because he has a D-minus average? You know that your best friend tends to be forgetful yet still you give her an important message, she forgets to relay it, why should you bother to be upset with her? Do you see the point? Expect what is to be expected of your loved ones. By experience and by your own assessment of each of them, you should at least have an idea of what to and what not to expect.

With that in mind, you will be equipped to make choices when dealing with your loved ones, that will be more compatible with their individual capabilities. Note though, that expecting the behavior of others does not necessarily mean accepting it. Whatever changes or adjustments can be made for the betterment of the person, by all means, be of assistance in doing so. By expecting the behavior you are simply accepting the fact that up until *that moment*, it would be unreasonable for you to expect otherwise.

Make Yourself Available to Your Loved Ones

The greatest gift is a portion of thyself.

Ralph Waldo Emerson

In this crazy world of anxious care, it is easy for you to get so caught up in getting things done that you lose sight of the more important things in life. Like that of tending to the needs of your loved ones. We all have needs, spoken and unspoken. When you truly love someone, you will, as best as you can, seek to discern what both are in his case. After discerning what these needs are, you should want to make yourself available to him with a view to assisting in his meeting them. You should sometimes take the initiative in addressing any difficulty you sense your loved ones may be experiencing and be there to help them with it as best as you reasonably can.

Because it is absolutely important to see to it that *your own* needs are sufficiently taken care of, sometimes it will call for great sacrifice on your part to make yourself available to others. But you can then, in each case, use your own discernment to determine how great a sacrifice you are in a position to make. While doing this though, bear in mind these words by Royce W. Duncan: 'Giving pleasure to a single heart by a single act will produce a joy in you that can never be replaced.'

Ways in which you can make yourself available to your loved ones include: offering to do favors for them; giving them phone calls when you can, even just to say hi; returning their calls as soon as possible; inviting them to spend time with you, even for short periods doing simple things; effectively listening to them. Effectively listening to your loved ones is one of the most important ways of making yourself available to them. For this reason I would like to expand a little on how you can do so.

Effectively listening to your loved ones means that you become absorbed in what they are saying, not allowing your mind to wander. You zero in on them giving them your undivided attention. You should look directly at them, observe their body language and listen to what they do not say. You should be careful however, that you do not concentrate too much on trying to do all these things or on trying to decide on how you will respond. This will be distracting to you. You should just allow yourself to participate in their feelings and your best responses will come naturally. Note however that while you love these persons and you want to help them, *you can not take responsibility for them or for their feelings*. You should not feel guilty if after you have done your reasonable best to help, there is no apparent progress. You would have already done your part by making yourself available to them in an effort to help. Let's talk a little bit more about making yourself available to your loved ones with a view to offering to them comfort or emotional support.

Insight on Mastering Empathy When Offering Emotional Support

Like the key needed to open a deep heavy safe, empathy is what is needed to open a deep and heavy heart. Empathy is the ability to identify with a person and so be able to participate in his thoughts and feelings. It is by this ability that we become sensitized to the needs of others, and so be in the best position to cater to those needs.

So what are some ways in which you can develop and exercise empathy when offering emotional support? To explore this let us look at an applicable illustration. Let us say someone comes to you feeling severely distressed by a problem or combination of problems and so is seeking comfort and advice.

The first thing you need to do is to build a basic psychological profile of this person. If he is not someone you are very familiar with, in order to do this you may need to ask him some general questions that will give you more or less an idea of where he is coming from psychologically. Perhaps you may want to know a little about his immediate family, his background, the persons he presently lives with, his dominant interests and so on. Do not go about this in a formal or question-and-answer way. You can simply find out these things in a light, conversational and friendly way. If done correctly, it should also serve to make him even more at ease with you. If he is someone you are already familiar with, then all you need to do is, in a split second 'ring up' his profile in the back of your mind.

Now the next step to be taken is where real empathy comes into play. Remember, the key to getting this person to open up to you and for you to really be effective in helping him, is for you to first *identify* with him. Now the absolute best way to do this is to try to find something in common between the two of you. Find in him some part of you, and although disturbing at times, find in you some part of him. You see, there must be a place to lodge the anchor before you dive *down into the deep ocean of some turbulent mind. By doing this you make it safe for yourself to go psychologically wherever he is going to take you, without getting lost or even injured on this journey. This lodged anchor or established common ground is what will serve as the landmark in finding your way safely back 'home'.*

Now while this person is speaking to you, look directly into his eyes. Look deep into them until you can almost see his need. Pay close attention to all his expressions. Not just to what they are but to how they are made. Is he rambling on and on? Perhaps it means he has so much to say and is desperate for someone to hear. Is he slow or hesitant in his speech? Perhaps it means he is not quite sure how to get out verbally what he needs to express, since he may be feeling a number of different emotions all at once. Also it could mean that he is not completely comfortable with having to talk about his problem – and if that is the case, you may need to be extra patient and try to, in some way, make him even more comfortable with you. Even his physical appearance can say a lot. Do his eyes look dull, or are they constantly downcast? It could mean that he has been carrying this burden by himself for a very long time. What about his posture? If he is slumping in his chair or loosely leaning on the armrests as if for extra support, it could be a sign that he's just about had it and needs all the support he can get.

Now as you observe and listen to this person and as you discern what his needs are, it becomes your turn to communicate to him that you are completely on his side. This should be done by your choice of words, tone of voice, by your questions (which should reflect your genuine interest), and even by your own posture which should be upright yet relaxed.

He needs to feel a connection between the two of you in a way that will make him see that he is not alone and that another human being is genuinely trying to understand his situation and has only his best interests at heart. In other words, the interchange between the two of you should not merely be an experience in which he talked, you listened and then offered straightforward practical suggestions. Instead it should be a meaningful psychological intercourse that results in his feeling a lightening of his burden, comfort and relief and in you feeling more aware and satisfied.

How will you know if the effect of your empathy is significantly felt and appreciated by him? When at the end of it all he smiles at you and perhaps asks to see you again.

Seek to Bring Out the Best In Your Loved Ones

In order to bring out the best in any person, one must first develop sensitivity to the unique needs of that one. One way to do this is to bear in mind that whenever you are relating to a person, you're not just relating to John Brown but you are relating to a combination of John Brown's family background, his childhood, his history, his weaknesses, his fears, his desires, his unmet needs, his strengths and even his experiences in the past few hours. All of which up until that point make up him. Because of this, you can never be quite sure of what his emotional and psychological states are like. The probability of them being exactly the same as when you related to him last is slim to none. This is because some time elapsed. With that time came new experiences and with those new experiences came adjustments, if even slight, to his present emotional or psychological state. When all this is borne in mind, it becomes easier to learn for ourselves how effectively we can bring out the best in each of our loved ones. For starters, here are a few examples of things that we can do.

1. *Discern what situations or subjects may be embarrassing to a person and try to avoid them.* Do your best so that people of all different kinds (Fat, slim; rich, poor; educated, uneducated) will be comfortable with being *themselves* around you.

2. *Encourage the habit of sincerely paying compliments to your loved ones.* While you don't want to overdo it, and so depreciate the value of your compliments, it is a loving thing to openly express your appreciation for some quality or feature of your loved one. Conscientiously look for unique characteristics of each person and let them know that you appreciate them.

3 *Encourage your loved ones to build on any talent or skill they may have.*

4 *Always wait for the right time before doing or saying something that may demand the time or attention of your loved one*. For instance, in the case of a woman, it would not at all be a loving thing for you to approach your tired, hungry husband with a complaint. If it can wait. Be patient. Let it wait. After all, 'a hungry man is an angry man' -- feed him first *and then* complain☺. And, in the case of a man, it would be equally unloving for you to even expect your exhausted wife to effectively perform all her wifely duties at the end of a demanding day. (Order out, wear an old shirt, or go take a cold shower.☺)

5 *Arrest and eradicate any resentment you may feel for a person.*

6 If for some reason you are upset or annoyed about something, try as best to *maintain your self-control* when it becomes time for you to relate to someone. Maintaining self-control will make you better able to avoid tones that are harsh, sarcastic, bitter, ones that connote suspicion or accusation. People have a funny way of detecting even the slightest hints of such tones and rather than bringing out their best, their reaction could bring out their worst.

7 *Avoid easily taking offense and taking every unpleasant comment personally.* Remember, 'words are nothing more than wind' and they can only mean as much to you if that is how *you choose* to perceive them.

8 *Express enthusiasm about the accomplishments of your loved ones, whether they are big or small.*

9 *Soften the tough things you might have to say.* From time to time we may need to, in an attempt to help a loved one, draw attention to a difficult or sensitive issue. Unfortunately, though we may have good intentions, our approach or our choice of words may bring across in the wrong way what we really intend to say. And, instead of ending up in encouragement, the conversation can result in hurt and resentment.

For such a situation, the effective use of euphemisms can be quite helpful. According to author Theodore M. Bernstein, "a euphemism is a word or phrase that affords a way of getting around saying something unpleasant. [They] are not fig leaves intended to hide something; they are diaphanous veils, intended to soften grossness or starkness." I admit, it sure would be a lot easier if we could just say what's on our mind just as it exists in our minds, but then we would be needlessly running the risk of hurting and possibly killing our loving relationships.

For argument's sake, what would be your approach to helping a loved one who say, suffers from a severe case of acne that is unsightly? Would you say, "Boy that acne sure is spoiling your good looks?" No. This would be a bitter blow to anyone's self esteem because the only two words he will hear in that entire comment are 'acne' and 'spoiling' and so your mentioning his 'good looks' would be ineffectual. He would only be embarrassed and maybe even offended. Instead, with a concerned tone, you could without sounding pitiful, express to him that you are aware of the anxiety and concern that his acne may possibly be causing him and then after reassuring him that his condition is not unique, find out what he has up until that point done to help the situation and then offer any additional advice. It would help to prepare for such a meeting by first doing a little research on the matter so that you can be equipped to offer valuable suggestions.

How about something a little more sensitive though? Say the issue of body odor. It seems to be the consensus that there is no kind way to tell someone that he or she smells unpleasantly. But there is. Try this. First, in a searching manner (not smiling) as if you're desperate to find a solution to *this* problem, ask your friend how *he* would approach his friend who suffers from an unpleasant body odor. Without interrupting him, allow him to respond. What you would actually be doing at this point, is to involve him in both roles. He would no doubt recognize that telling his friend about his problem is indeed a difficult thing to do, but he would at the same time recognize that it would be a necessary thing to do out of love for his friend. That way, when you do get around to telling him (based on *his* response) he would have already realized that it was not easy for you but also that you had purely loving intentions. It would also help for you to clearly attribute his problem to the actual cause which is the *bacteria itself*. Perhaps you could mention that for some persons it can increase at more rapid rates when certain kinds of foods are eaten. This is better, rather than implying that he is in someway unsanitary. True, this may very well be the case, but the point is, not to embarrass or upset him but to incite him to curative action. Yes, there is no issue so tough that a little imagination, empathy and *careful* choice of words can't soften.

10 *Maintain active relationships with your loved ones.* Surprise your loved ones with gifts; big or small it does not matter. Flowers are always nice. Pay them visits. Invite them over. Return their calls, especially when you say you will. Write them surprise letters or notes. Update them on your experiences and allow them to share theirs with you. The point is, avoid stagnating your loving relationships. Instead, encourage them to grow.

Express Love to the Physical Being

It must be established that the nurturing of the physical person is no less important than that of the psychological or emotional. Of course, the only real direct way of nurturing any physical being is by touch. Touch is profoundly essential to our growth as human beings, from infancy straight on to old age. Touch provides reassurance, warmth, acceptance, pleasure, comfort and a sense of security; all of which we desire of and for our loved ones. The language of touch is one we must become fluent in in order to completely communicate to our loved ones, our love for them.

Scientific experiments have revealed that touch deprivation almost always results in the stunting of physical and emotional growth. Consequently, this could stunt the growth of any relationship we may have with a victim of such.

Unfortunately, in our society, meaningful touching such as hugging, kissing, rubbing, caressing and cuddling is primarily reserved for coaxing the sick, conveying sympathy to the bereaved, or for sexual participation. Really, this is unhealthy, as it is the same as abandoning our natural instincts. We seem to suffer from some sort of contact phobia, which limits our touching, or our being touched, to our mates, children, very close family, friends, or pets. Sad to say, this is not even the case in all such relationships. Because we are very aware that there exists so many perverts and sexual offenders in our world, we naturally form a kind of protective mechanism that may cause us to withdraw from unexpected, but even innocent and meaningful touching, even from persons we know well. In a split second our subconscious minds may instruct us to be very conscious or suspicious of their touch.

Low self-esteem also plays a part in the inability to interpret innocent touching as being harmless and meaningful. Such a one might subconsciously think: "Why would he (or she) want to touch me?"

If you suspect that you are one of such persons who finds it difficult to accept or to give touch, even on occasions when it is not 'necessary,' if you wish to, you can be helped to exercise balance in this regard. If you start out by making conscious efforts to touch your loved ones more, the effects will be positive for all parties, as self images grow healthier, and mutual appreciation grows stronger. I am not here suggesting that you go around embracing and petting everyone you know. That, of course, would be out of order and very possibly dangerous. The nature of your various relationships differ and so obviously your levels of familiarity and hence the degree and nature of your touching with each of your loved ones should differ. For instance, the way you would touch say, your acquaintances likely would differ from the way you would touch your close friends. The way you physically handle your grandparents may differ from the way you would your younger, stronger relatives. Also, differences in forms and degrees of touching would exist when dealing with a member of the opposite sex to whom you are not married, as opposed to someone to whom you are. Discernment and caution are key when dealing with such delicate matters.

We can all trust our instincts and allow them to serve as our guides in this respect. They will tell us just how far to go with each person, or whether to touch them or allow them to touch us at all. Our *instincts* rather than our *conscious minds* will also prevent us from causing offense or arousing in a person a sense of violation or suspicion rather than a sense of appreciation. All this is essential to loving our loved ones; expressing appreciation for their physical beings rather than succumbing to the fear of innocently, meaningfully touching them. In closing this point, let me get poetic on you.

Whether it's a peck on the cheek or a gentle licking of the face, a simple pat on the back or a warm embrace, a casual handshake or a massaging of any place, touching is loving *once there is no disgrace.* ☺

Concluding Remarks

The five platinum keys here discussed reveal just a *part* of what it takes to master the delicate art of loving your loved ones. The fact that it is just a *part* should not dissuade you though, but should only enhance your awareness and respect for the beauty of human life. In particular those of your loved ones. Based on what you've just read, you, like my friend mentioned at the outset, may perceive the act of effectively loving your loved ones to be a difficult task. However, as you heighten your own self-esteem, broaden your understanding and appreciation of others and deepen your own sense of self-love and self-security, your natural capability to completely, effectively love your loved ones will shine through without much conscious effort on your part. No doubt, a significant part of developing this self-love and appreciation is by taking care of *your own* physical being. This we'll now consider in the concluding chapter.

Dedicated to my beloved friend Ruff.

Chapter Nine

Platinum Keys To Caring For Your Physical Being

I hardly believe that I need to offer an extensive discussion on the advantages or the importance of keeping good health. Especially in this modern age of advanced illnesses and disorders, chemical pollution and with the proliferation of so many different strains of viral and bacterial infections, it is agreed and accepted by most that not paying special attention to personal health is not only unwise but also detrimental to one's life.

Taking a serious yet balanced approach to our health care is a sign of respect to our physical beings. It shows that we take our responsibility to our bodies seriously and that we place high value on the gift of human life. Consequently, the quality of our lives will be enriched as we will benefit not just physically, but emotionally, psychologically, mentally and socially as well.

Now, I am not a health care professional, but I will just list a few platinum health keys taken from basic general knowledge that may serve as reminders and as incitement to you. Realistically, you may not be able to apply *all* of them at all times, but continuously making yourself aware of them will move you closer towards applying them. Let's now take a look at them.

1 Understand *why* you need to be healthier and cultivate the personal desire to be that way.

2 Get at least a basic education in nutrition.

3 Apply what you learn; which would mean eating nutritious foods and avoiding junk foods. Also, it would mean avoiding the excessive eating of foods with harmful chemicals, such as foods with artificial preservatives, coloring, or flavoring. Also burned, greasy or yeasty foods.

4 Eat regularly, but moderately.

5 Drink purified water. (It may be cheaper to buy yourself a water filter instead of regularly purchasing bottled water.)

6 Exercise regularly. Aerobics, stretches and even weight-lifting if you can. Also, try and play a fun active sport such as tennis, swimming, or basketball.

7 Get advice on the best quality brands of vitamin and mineral supplements and take them regularly. You may think you cannot afford them, but remember, it is more than a worthwhile investment.

8 Get de-wormed at least twice per year.

9 Avoid becoming gassy or bloated. This can be done by avoiding prolonged periods without eating and by avoiding foods and drinks that tend to cause excessive gas.

10 Maintain good personal hygiene. For instance, take regular baths. See to it that your teeth, ears, hair and nails are kept clean. Wear fresh clothing and keep all your personal items, such as toothbrushes and washcloths, *personal.*

11 Learn massage therapy, reflexology or any other from of touch therapy. You will find it to be quite beneficial. For instance I will show you how you can get rid of a headache and an upset stomach in less than 30 seconds using only reflexology.

For A Headache

Using the ball of your right thumb, find the point of intersection between the base of your left thumb and the base of your left index finger. Apply pressure to this point. It should be noticeably tender or painful but not unbearably so. Hold for a few seconds or squeeze pulsingly until there is significant relief of your headache. Switch hands and repeat the procedure if necessary.

For An Upset Stomach

a) Place your right wrist, with the palm of your hand facing downwards, upon your right knee cap.

b) Without shifting your wrist, bring your hand down to hold your leg (that should be just below your knee or at your upper shin).

c) Clutch your leg so that your right thumb will be on the left side of your shin and your four fingers on the right.

d) Now pay attention to the points that your **four fingers** are touching. Those are the points you should now apply pressure to by gripping your leg tightly. Focus on the point that is most tender or painful. Again, you can squeeze pulsingly if you desire until there is a significant relief of your upset stomach.

e) Switch legs and repeat the procedure if necessary. (NB: Whichever leg you use, the reflex points are situated on the *outer side* of the leg.)

Congratulations! You have just learned how to use your fingers to replace aspirins and antacids. Try it on yourself and on others while bearing in mind that this is just a small sample of the effective use of touch therapy. There is so much more you can learn.

12 Get or give yourself a form of touch therapy as often as you are able to.

13 Maintain good sleeping habits. For instance, sleep in a surrounding that makes you feel secure. It should also be quiet and dark. Make sure your bed is firm, and if you can, get one of those pillows that are designed to support your neck. Even if you slept poorly the night before, do not take naps late in the day. Try to remain awake and then retire at your usual time. Avoid caffeine, exercise, alcohol and large meals just before bedtime. Also, do not use your bed for reading, studying or for watching television.

14 Abandon all forms of substance addiction. (see Chapter Seven)

15 Do not allow any kind of skin or nail fungus to grow. Take appropriate action to eliminate any of such.

16 Maintain clean surroundings. For instance, if you have carpeting, vacuum it regularly. If you use fans, keep the blades clean. Get an air filter if you can. Disinfect regularly, areas where food is usually present and keep all your sponges and dishcloths clean.

17 Detox yourself at least once per year.

18 Keep your body's pH as alkaline as possible. Scientists believe that this makes your system less accommodative to viruses, bacteria and other germs and hence to infections. You can do this by eating grapefruits or drinking lime water. (Not oranges which have high levels of fructose which tend to promote yeast.)

19 Treat all cavities or other oral problems you might have.

20 Keep your throat clean. Gargle with diluted Hydrogen Peroxide or Apple Cider Vinegar.

21 Care for your beautiful eyes. For instance, if you think you need glasses, don't wait long to see a doctor. Work in proper lighting. Do not sit too close to your TV or your computer screen.

22 Avoid disorientation or constipation. Eat foods with lots of roughage such as cabbage, spinach and carrots and drink lots of pure water. Prune juice is also very effective for solving this problem.

23 Cultivate a healthy interest in learning different ways of taking care of your health.

24 If you happen to be suffering with a serious illness, learn as much as you can about it, think of ways to maintain your sense of humor and educate as many about it as possible so that they may be better able to respond to your needs. Avoid feeling sorry for yourself and continue to show love and kindness to others.

25 Shun negative thinking and avoid prolonged uptightness, envy, anger, fear, guilt and worry.

26 Listen to your body and respond to what you hear.

27 Find satisfaction in your job or in your other duties.

28 Develop and display compassion for all living things.

29 Take long meaningful vacations. If they cannot be long, at least make them meaningful.

30 Sing out loud your favorite songs.

31 If you are not allergic and if you have suitable circumstances, own a pet.

32 Apply as many of these suggestions as you can.

My Final Word

Certainly, we have discussed together some very personal and important issues. Issues that affect all of us and ones that we must comfortably resolve in our minds and hearts in order to be truly advanced. As the music fades and our dance comes to an end, it is my hope that we both right now, feel a deep sense of stimulation and motivation.

There is something else that I must encourage you to do, however. Not only must you seek to familiarize yourself with suggestions that will aid in your advancement, but also you must *seriously act* on such suggestions. There is a wise old Oriental saying that goes like this:

> *You see -- you remember*
> *You hear -- you forget*
> *You* **do** -- *you* **understand**.

Before I go, I have one final word of caution. As you continue to progress in personal advancement, *be careful not to think too much of yourself*. Be careful that you do not get so wrapped up in advancing yourself that you end up insulating yourself, only to gradually become inhumane and thus missing the point of living altogether as so many others have.

I sincerely wish you all the best in every positive thing you do. Possibly, we will meet again, but for now I must say, with a graceful curtsy, it was indeed a pleasure waltzing with you.

Acknowledgements

This book is based on data accumulated throughout my entire life, thus far. Because of this, it is impossible for me to acknowledge everyone who contributed to it and so I hope that it suffices to just thank everyone that I know.

I would especially though like to thank my father Steve, the most brilliant man I know, for his enduring strength and for the wisdom he continues to impart to me. Also my mother Bobette, for her undying love and faith in me. My big brother Steven for being my best friend, and my little sister Shari, for keeping me in line. Also Grandpa John and Grandma Pearle, thank you so much.

I also would like to thank you Tracey-Ann Kettle for all our long, wonderful 2am. talks. You are very special to me. Also Beverley Evans, Karen Riettie, Joyce Jones, Lesa Elliott, Hayden and Yvonne Jordan, Keith and Lydia Medina and Timothy and Ruth Harley -- my adopted big brother and sister. Thank you Carl Cameron, Alison Richardson, Cheryl Bonnick, the Hallimans, Cleve Bowen, Gordon D'Quesnay,

Sharon Gibson, Jacqueline O'Brien, Gaye Burke, Eugene Harris and Dr. Elsa Leo-Rayne. Gloria Malcolm -- thanks a million.

A special gracias to my family the Davis' and the Coleys for all your love and support. Also, to Michael Bonnick, not only for you priceless friendship but also for wonderfully producing my pictorial illustrations. Cheryl, Althea, Alicia, Natalee, Priya, Trudy, and Gillian, I thank you too.

Finally, I wish to thank all my former teachers, particularly Miss Cunningham, Mrs. Wilson, Miss Bartley, Miss Jarrett, Mr. Davis, Miss Swearing and Mrs. Joy Bryan.

For those who, because of space, I failed to mention, I offer my sincere regrets and to you special ones I say thank you, thank you, thank you!